The Art of
PRAYER

Kenneth E. Hagin

Unless otherwise indicated, all Scripture quotations in this volume are from the *King James Version* of the Bible.

Fourth Edition
Fifth Printing 1996

ISBN 0-89276-518-6

In the U.S. write:
Kenneth Hagin Ministries
P.O. Box 50126
Tulsa, OK 74150-0126

In Canada write:
Kenneth Hagin Ministries
P.O. Box 335, Station D,
Etobicoke (Toronto), Ontario
Canada, M9A 4X3

BOOKS BY KENNETH E. HAGIN

The Triumphant Church: Dominion Over All the Powers of Darkness
Healing Scriptures
Mountain-Moving Faith
Love: The Way to Victory
Biblical Keys to Financial Prosperity
The Price Is Not Greater Than God's Grace (Mrs. Oretha Hagin)

MINIBOOKS (A partial listing)

* The New Birth
* Why Tongues?
* In Him
* God's Medicine
* You Can Have What You Say
* Don't Blame God
* Words
  Plead Your Case
* How To Keep Your Healing
  The Bible Way To Receive the Holy Spirit
  I Went to Hell
  How To Walk in Love
  The Precious Blood of Jesus
* Love Never Fails
  How God Taught Me About Prosperity

BOOKS BY KENNETH HAGIN JR.

* Man's Impossibility — God's Possibility
  Because of Jesus
  How To Make the Dream God Gave You Come True
  The Life of Obedience
  Forget Not!
  God's Irresistible Word
  Healing: Forever Settled
  Don't Quit! Your Faith Will See You Through
  The Untapped Power in Praise
  Listen to Your Heart
  What Comes After Faith?
  Speak to Your Mountain!
  Come Out of the Valley!
  It's Your Move!
  God's Victory Plan
  Another Look at Faith

MINIBOOKS (A partial listing)

* Faith Worketh by Love
* Seven Hindrances to Healing
* The Past Tense of God's Word
  Faith Takes Back What the Devil's Stolen
  How To Be a Success in Life
  Get Acquainted With God
  Unforgiveness
  Ministering to the Brokenhearted

*These titles are also available in Spanish. Information about other foreign translations of several of the above titles (i.e., Finnish, French, German, Indonesian, Polish, Russian, etc.) may be obtained by writing to: Kenneth Hagin Ministries, P.O. Box 50126, Tulsa, Oklahoma 74150-0126.

Contents

Foreword

Acknowledgment

Foreword

All of us are continually growing in our knowledge of God and in our understanding of His Word. Since this book was first released under the title *The Art of Intercession*, my study of God's Word has brought new understanding in the area of prayer. Because of insights gained where the prayers of intercession and supplication are concerned, I felt it was no longer appropriate to call this book, *The Art of Intercession*. Intercession is only one type of prayer. Actually, supplication covers a broader spectrum of prayer than does intercession, but the scope of this book involves even more than just these two kinds of prayer. For this reason, I asked our editors to change the name of the book to *The Art of Prayer*. This re-edited version reflects some of the additional illumination I have received over the last few years. My desire is that this book will stir believers to commit themselves to prayer so that the purpose of God can be consummated in the earth.

Acknowledgment

Reverend Wilford H. Reidt of Kennewick, Washington, was an outstanding Bible teacher. Wilford's wife, Gertrude, was the daughter of John G. Lake, well-known apostle of faith in the early days of this century. The Reidts were greatly used by God for many years in the area of prayer before they both went home to be with the Lord.

Wilford's teachings on the subject of prayer reveal a depth of knowledge that could only have been gained from years of experience in prayer. I was so impressed with his study outline and comments on the subject of prayer that I asked his permission to use his materials in this book to the glory of God.

We believe that God will use this book to raise up and train a great number of people who know how to pray and who will be at the forefront of the work of the Lord in these last days. Brother Reidt gave me permission to use his material and his remarks appear throughout the book in recognizable type.

Chapter 1
Why Pray?

Years ago I read a statement John Wesley made and it stayed with me. Wesley said, *"It seems God is limited by our prayer life — that He can do nothing for humanity unless someone asks Him."*

A while later, in 1949, I was reading after another writer who made that same statement. But this fellow added, *"Why this is, I do not know."*

"Why doesn't he know?" I asked. Then I found out I didn't know either.

Yet if Wesley's statement is correct — and it seems to be as you read through the Bible — then we who are to pray should know more about it.

I began to examine the Bible to find out why, if God wants to do something for humanity, He cannot unless somebody asks Him. I found the answer through study of God's Word.

You see, though some people have built up "spiritual air castles" that God is running everything in this world, He is not.

During the Vietnam War a nationally syndicated newspaper columnist began one column by stating that he was not a Christian. He said that he was not an atheist because the atheist says there is no God.

"I suppose you would classify me an agnostic," he wrote. "The agnostic says there may be a God, but if there is, I don't know it. Actually, I am prone to believe there is a Supreme Being. I do not believe that every-

1

thing here just happened. I believe there is a Creator somewhere.

"But I have never read the Bible. I do not attend church. One reason I don't is that what the Christians say about God doesn't agree with what I think a Creator should be, nor with what I can see of Him in nature.

"Even ministers say, 'God has everything under control. He's running everything.'

"Well, if He is, He sure has things in a mess. People are killing each other. Little children are dying. Little children are hungry. Women are suffering. There are wars everywhere.

"If God has everything under control, do you mean God is running those wars?"

Even an unregenerate columnist knew that wasn't right.

God is not ruling in this world. He is not ruling on the earth.

Thank God, He will one day!

But right now His will is not being carried out on the earth, except in the lives of those who surrender to Him.

That is easy to see if you will accept what the Bible says. The Bible says that God is not willing that any should perish, but that all should come to repentance (2 Peter 3:9). It is obvious that His will concerning the salvation of all men is not being carried out.

When individuals accept the Lord Jesus Christ as their Savior, it is carried out in their lives. But if God were running things and pushing His will off on people, since He is not willing that any should perish, He would make everybody get saved today and we would go into the Millennium tomorrow.

As I examined God's Word for the "why" behind John Wesley's statement, I saw a truth I had never seen before, though I had been in the ministry many years.

As I asked the Lord about it, He said to me, "Go back to the Book of Beginnings."

I knew He meant the Book of Genesis. I reread it. I had read it many times. I had heard it taught as a Sunday School boy. But I saw it in a different light this time.

I saw that God made the world and the fullness thereof. He made His man, Adam.

Then He said, "Adam, I give you dominion over all the work of my hands" (Gen. 1:26,27; Ps. 8:6).

God did not say, "I am going to dominate through you."

He said, "I give you dominion over all the work of my hands." Therefore Adam had dominion upon this earth and in this world. He was originally, in a sense, god of this world.

But Satan came and lied to Adam. Adam committed high treason and sold out to Satan. Then Satan became the god of this world.

Second Corinthians 4:4 calls Satan "the god of this world." As such, he has dominion. Where? In this world.

He will have that dominion, he will be god of this world, until Adam's lease runs out.

God cannot legally and justly move in and take away that dominion from the devil. The devil has dominion here. He has a legal right because he has Adam's lease. And God cannot do anything unless somebody down here asks Him.

Chapter 2
Various Kinds of Prayer

Praying always with all prayer and supplication in the Spirit, and watching thereunto with all perseverance and supplication for all saints.
                                                    — Ephesians 6:18

Notice that says, *"Praying . . . with ALL prayer. . . ."*

The *Amplified* translation reads, "Pray . . . with ALL [MANNER of] prayer. . . ."

Another translation reads, "Praying with ALL KINDS of prayer. . . ."

But the translation that really strikes a note in my own spirit is Goodspeed's. It reads, "Use EVERY KIND of prayer and entreaty, and at every opportunity pray in the Spirit. . . ." The Bible teaches several kinds of prayer — and the different rules governing them.

The church world makes a mistake in not differentiating between those different kinds of praying. We simply put all prayer in the same sack and shake it all out together. Many prayers are not working because people are using the wrong rules and laws.

In the field of sports, for instance, we have baseball, basketball, football, golf, tennis, etc. These are all kinds of sports — but they are not all played by the same rules.

Wouldn't it be confusing to play a baseball game with football rules, or vice versa?

The reason people are confused and have a prayer

problem is that they have their rules and laws all mixed up together. They take rules which govern one kind of praying and try to apply them to other kinds of praying.

Speaking illustratively, they've got football, baseball, basketball, golf, and tennis rules supposedly all working together. They are confused. And so is their prayer life.

One common misconception people have is they think they should conclude every prayer with the words, "If it be Thy will." They claim that is how Jesus prayed. However, Jesus prayed this way on only one occasion that is recorded in Scripture. That was in the Garden of Gethsemane when He prayed *the prayer of consecration.*

When they attempt to pray *the prayer of faith* (the prayer of petition, the prayer to change things), they conclude it with "if it be Thy will." And their prayer is hindered because they are uncertain of His will — His Word.

They may say, "I don't understand why that didn't work." That would be like saying at a football game, "I don't see why someone doesn't hit a home run."

Don't be confused. Go to the Rulebook! Go to the Bible and see how to pray.

I will list here several kinds of prayers the Bible teaches. However, I cannot go into detail on all of them in this book. (I do have books on prayer which deal with them in more detail.)

The Prayer of Faith: the prayer of petition, the prayer to change things (Matt. 21:22; Mark 11:24). This prayer, always to be based on God's revealed will in His Word, never contains an "if."

The Prayer of Consecration: the prayer of consecration and dedication of our lives for God's use — to go anywhere and do anything. In this prayer we pray, "If it be Thy will" (Luke 22:42).

The Prayer of Commitment: casting your cares upon the Lord in prayer (1 Peter 5:7).

The Prayer of Worship (Luke 24:52,53; Acts 13:1-4).

The Prayer of Agreement (Matt. 18:18-20).

Prayer in the Spirit: praying in tongues (1 Cor. 14:14,15).

United Prayer (Acts 4:23-31).

The Prayer of Supplication.

Intercessory Prayer.

The last two types of prayer are primarily covered in the next two chapters.

(For additional teaching on different types of prayer, please *see* Brother Hagin's book, *Prevailing Prayer to Peace.*)

Chapter 3
Supplication Defined

The nature of supplication is much more heartfelt than a casual request. The word "supplication" means a *humble, earnest entreaty* or *request*. If a request is not made in a heartfelt, fervent, and earnest manner, it would not be supplication.

For Whom Can Supplication Be Made?

First, we pray the prayer of supplication for ourselves concerning both natural and spiritual needs.

PHILIPPIANS 4:6
6   Be careful for nothing; but in every thing by prayer and SUPPLICATION with thanksgiving let your requests be made known unto God.

Second, we pray the prayer of supplication for God's people — for believers or all saints.

EPHESIANS 6:18
18   Praying always with all prayer and SUPPLICATION in the Spirit, and watching thereunto with all perseverance and SUPPLICATION for ALL SAINTS.

Third, we are to pray the prayer of supplication for all men and for those who are in authority. That would include unbelievers as well.

1 TIMOTHY 2:1,2
1   I exhort therefore, that, first of all, SUPPLICATIONS, prayers, intercessions, and giving of thanks, be

made for ALL MEN;
2   For kings, and for all that are in authority; that we
may lead a quiet and peaceable life in all godliness and
honesty.

For What Can Supplication Be Made?

One of the things for which supplication can be made
is for laborers to be sent into God's harvest.

MATTHEW 9:37,38
**37 Then saith he unto his disciples, The harvest truly
is plenteous, but the labourers are few;
38 PRAY ye therefore the Lord of the harvest, that he
will send forth labourers into his harvest.**

The word translated as "pray" in verse 38 involves
the idea of an urgent and necessary request presented
with fervency and desire.

Supplication can also be made for the rain of God's
Spirit to be poured out upon the earth.

ZECHARIAH 10:1
**1   ASK ye of the Lord rain in the time of the latter
rain; so the Lord shall make bright clouds, and give
them showers of rain, to every one grass in the field.**

The word translated as "ask" in this verse means *to
desire, to ask earnestly*, and *to require*.

JAMES 5:7,16-18
**7   Be patient therefore, brethren, unto the coming of
the Lord. Behold, the husbandman waiteth for the precious fruit of the earth, and hath long patience for it,
until he receive the early and latter rain. . . .
16 Confess your faults one to another, and pray one for**

another, that ye may be healed. The effectual fervent
prayer of a righteous man availeth much.
17 Elias was a man subject to like passions as we are,
and he prayed earnestly that it might not rain: and it
rained not on the earth by the space of three years and
six months.
18 And he prayed again, and the heaven gave rain, and
the earth brought forth her fruit.

JAMES 5:16 *(Amplified)*
16 Confess to one another therefore your faults — your
slips, your false steps, your offenses, your sins; and
pray [also] for one another, that you may be healed and
restored — to a spiritual tone of mind and heart. The
earnest (heartfelt, continued) prayer of a righteous
man makes tremendous power available — dynamic in
its working.

Notice the characteristics of supplication in these
verses — it is fervent, earnest, heartfelt, and continued.
Such prayer makes tremendous power available!

We can also offer the prayer of supplication to obtain
forgiveness.

DANIEL 9:2,3,17,18
2 In the first year of his reign I Daniel understood by
books the number of the years, whereof the word of the
Lord came to Jeremiah the prophet, that he would
accomplish seventy years in the desolations of
Jerusalem.
3 And I set my face unto the Lord God, to seek by
prayer and SUPPLICATIONS, with fasting, and sack-
cloth, and ashes. . . .
17 Now therefore, O our God, hear the prayer of thy
servant, and his SUPPLICATIONS, and cause thy face
to shine upon thy sanctuary that is desolate, for the
Lord's sake.

18 O my God, incline thine ear, and hear; open thine eyes, and behold our desolations, and the city which is called by thy name: for we do not present our SUPPLI-CATIONS before thee for our righteousnesses, but for thy great mercies.

Here we see Daniel earnestly confessing his own sins and the sins of his people. Repenting and confessing your sins is done by means of the prayer of supplication.

Finally, we pray the prayer of supplication to lift up the spiritual needs of others. The words "prayer" or "pray" in the following verses literally mean supplication or earnest prayer.

EPHESIANS 1:16
16 Cease not to give thanks for you, making mention of you in my PRAYERS.

PHILIPPIANS 1:9
9 And this I PRAY, that your love may abound yet more and more in knowledge and in all judgment.

COLOSSIANS 1:9
9 For this cause we also, since the day we heard it, do not cease to PRAY for you, and to desire that ye might be filled with the knowledge of his will in all wisdom and spiritual understanding.

COLOSSIANS 4:12
12 Epaphras, who is one of you, a servant of Christ, saluteth you, always labouring fervently for you in PRAYERS, that ye may stand perfect and complete in all the will of God.

In these prayers Paul prayed and recorded in the epistles, he was making reference to supplication.

Chapter 4
Intercession Defined

The purpose of defining intercession or any other kind of prayer is not to limit or confine prayer to a set of rules and regulations, but to give a better understanding of what the Bible teaches about each type of prayer. Equipped with such knowledge, the believer can cooperate more fully with the Holy Spirit because the Holy Spirit always works in conjunction with the Word.

Many people have lost the true spirit of prayer by becoming legalistic and clinical in their praying. It's more important to recognize and learn to flow with the Holy Spirit in prayer than merely to know correct prayer terminology.

For a long time, almost all prayer was called "intercession," or it was thought that intercession was the only effective kind of praying. But in reality, the most effective prayer is the prayer the Holy Spirit inspires which is *needed at the moment* — whether it is the prayer of agreement, the prayer of faith, the prayer of praise and worship, or some other type of prayer. Often different kinds of prayer will work together much like the fingers on a hand. For instance, supplication, which is an earnest, heartfelt request, is used in intercession.

Briefly defined, intercession is standing in the gap in prayer between a person or persons, who have provoked judgment upon themselves through their wrongdoing, and the actual execution of that judgment. Or to put it more simply, intercession is prayer to hold back judgment. To be

effective, intercession needs to be made at the prompting
of and under the direction of the Holy Spirit.

So that we can better understand intercession, let's
examine some instances in Scripture when intercession
was made.

GENESIS 18:16-33
16 And the men rose up from thence, and looked
toward Sodom: and Abraham went with them to bring
them on the way.
17 And the Lord said, Shall I hide from Abraham that
thing which I do;
18 Seeing that Abraham shall surely become a great
and mighty nation, and all the nations of the earth
shall be blessed in him?
19 For I know him, that he will command his children
and his household after him, and they shall keep the
way of the Lord, to do justice and judgment; that the
Lord may bring upon Abraham that which he hath spoken of him.
20 And the Lord said, Because the cry of Sodom and
Gomorrah is great, and because their sin is very
grievous;
21 I will go down now, and see whether they have done
altogether according to the cry of it, which is come
unto me; and if not, I will know.
22 And the men turned their faces from thence, and
went toward Sodom: but Abraham stood yet before the
Lord.
23 And Abraham drew near, and said, Wilt thou also
destroy the righteous with the wicked?
24 Peradventure there be fifty righteous within the
city: wilt thou also destroy and not spare the place for
the fifty righteous that are therein?
25 That be far from thee to do after this manner, to
slay the righteous with the wicked: and that the righteous should be as the wicked, that be far from thee:

Shall not the Judge of all the earth do right?
26 And the Lord said, If I find in Sodom fifty righteous within the city, then I will spare all the place for their sakes.
27 And Abraham answered and said, Behold now, I have taken upon me to speak unto the Lord, which am but dust and ashes:
28 Peradventure there shall lack five of the fifty righteous: wilt thou destroy all the city for lack of five? And he said, If I find there forty and five, I will not destroy it.
29 And he spake unto him yet again, and said, Peradventure there shall be forty found there. And he said, I will not do it for forty's sake.
30 And he said unto him, Oh let not the Lord be angry, and I will speak: Peradventure there shall thirty be found there. And he said, I will not do it, if I find thirty there.
31 And he said, Behold now, I have taken upon me to speak unto the Lord: Peradventure there shall be twenty found there. And he said, I will not destroy it for twenty's sake.
32 And he said, Oh let not the Lord be angry, and I will speak yet but this once: Peradventure ten shall be found there. And he said, I will not destroy it for ten's sake.
33 And the Lord went his way, as soon as he had left communing with Abraham: and Abraham returned unto his place.

Abraham's prayer for Sodom and Gomorrah is a clear example of the prayer of intercession. There is an important thing we need to note from this biblical account. God mentions a cry that arose from Sodom and Gomorrah in verses 20 and 21.

Smith Wigglesworth said once that there is something about faith that will cause God to pass over a million people just to get to one person who is in faith. You see, the cry of faith will bring God on the scene. The cry of faith *invokes* a blessing. The word "invoke" means *to call forth, to put into operation,* or *to bring about.*

But sin also cries out to God and brings Him on the scene. Rather than *invoking* God, sin *provokes* God. The word "provoke" means *to incite to anger, to call forth, to bring on,* and *to stir up on purpose.* Sin provokes God and calls forth wrath and judgment.

Time and again in Scripture we read where Israel provoked God to anger, and judgment came. God does not delight in seeing people receive judgment. According to Micah 7:18, God delights in mercy.

> **MICAH 7:18**
> **18 Who is a God like unto thee, that pardoneth iniquity, and passeth by the transgression of the remnant of his heritage? he retaineth not his anger for ever, because he delighteth in mercy.**

> **EZEKIEL 33:11**
> **11 Say unto them, As I live, saith the Lord God, I have no pleasure in the death of the wicked; but that the wicked turn from his way and live: turn ye, turn ye from your evil ways; for why will ye die, O house of Israel?**

However, if the ones who have sinned and provoked judgment upon themselves do not turn and repent, the only hope for judgment to be averted is for someone to stand in the gap for them and make intercession.

> **EZEKIEL 22:30,31**
> **30 And I sought for a man among them, that should make up the hedge, and stand in the gap before me for the land, that I should not destroy it: but I found none.**

31 Therefore have I poured out mine indignation upon them; I have consumed them with the fire of my wrath: their own way have I recompensed upon their heads, saith the Lord God.

In these verses we can see that God Himself sought for someone to stand in the gap for the land. But when no one was found, judgment was poured out. It is important to notice what God's will was in this matter. God's will was that someone stand in the gap so the land would not be destroyed. We need to equip ourselves with an understanding of God's will when we go before Him to make intercession on behalf of others. God's highest and best is that people turn to Him and live.

Second Peter 3:9 further enforces God's will concerning all men.

2 PETER 3:9
9 The Lord is not slack concerning his promise, as some men count slackness; but is longsuffering to us-ward, not willing that any should perish, but that all should come to repentance.

There were two occasions when Moses had to stand in the gap or make intercession for the children of Israel who had provoked God by their idolatry and sin:

NUMBERS 14:11-19
11 And the Lord said unto Moses, How long will this people provoke me? and how long will it be ere they believe me, for all the signs which I have shewed among them?
12 I will smite them with the pestilence, and disinherit them, and will make of thee a greater nation and mightier than they.

13 And Moses said unto the Lord, Then the Egyptians
shall hear it, (for thou broughtest up this people in thy
might from among them;)
14 And they will tell it to the inhabitants of this land:
for they have heard that thou Lord art among this people, that thou Lord art seen face to face, and that thy
cloud standeth over them, and that thou goest before
them, by day time in a pillar of a cloud, and in a pillar
of fire by night.
15 Now if thou shalt kill all this people as one man,
then the nations which have heard the fame of thee
will speak, saying,
16 Because the Lord was not able to bring this people
into the land which he sware unto them, therefore he
hath slain them in the wilderness.
17 And now, I beseech thee, let the power of my Lord
be great, according as thou hast spoken, saying,
18 The Lord is longsuffering, and of great mercy, for-
giving iniquity and transgression, and by no means
clearing the guilty, visiting the iniquity of the fathers
upon the children unto the third and fourth genera-
tion.
19 Pardon, I beseech thee, the iniquity of this people
according unto the greatness of thy mercy, and as thou
hast forgiven this people, from Egypt even until now.

EXODUS 32:7-14
7   And the Lord said unto Moses, Go, get thee down;
for thy people, which thou broughtest out of the land of
Egypt, have corrupted themselves:
8   They have turned aside quickly out of the way
which I commanded them: they have made them a
molten calf, and have worshipped it, and have sacri-
ficed thereunto, and said, These be thy gods, O Israel,
which have brought thee up out of the land of Egypt.
9   And the Lord said unto Moses, I have seen this
people, and, behold, it is a stiffnecked people:
10 Now therefore let me alone, that my wrath may wax

hot against them, and that I may consume them: and I will make of thee a great nation.
11 And Moses besought the Lord his God, and said, Lord, why doth thy wrath wax hot against thy people, which thou hast brought forth out of the land of Egypt with great power, and with a mighty hand?
12 Wherefore should the Egyptians speak, and say, For mischief did he bring them out, to slay them in the mountains, and to consume them from the face of the earth? Turn from thy fierce wrath, and repent of this evil against thy people.
13 Remember Abraham, Isaac, and Israel, thy servants, to whom thou swarest by thine own self, and saidst unto them, I will multiply your seed as the stars of heaven, and all this land that I have spoken of will I give unto your seed, and they shall inherit it for ever.
14 And the Lord repented of the evil which he thought to do unto his people.

Psalm 106 gives further insight into the importance of Moses' intercessory prayers in withholding judgment from the children of Israel. Note especially verse 23:

PSALM 106:23
23 Therefore he said that he would destroy them, had not Moses his chosen stood before him in the breach, to turn away his wrath, lest he should destroy them.

We can see from this verse that had Moses not stood in the gap for Israel, they would surely have been destroyed in judgment.

However, the most precious and outstanding example of an intercessor is our Lord Jesus who stood in the gap for us and who now intercedes for us at the Father's right hand. In the next two chapters we will look at His intercessory role on our behalf.

Chapter 5
Man's Need for an Intercessor

*For he is not a man, as I am, that I should
answer him, and we should come together in judgment. Neither is there any days man betwixt us,
that might lay his hand upon us both.*

— Job 9:32,33

The marginal rendering in my *King James* reference
Bible for the word translated "days man" is "umpire."
Another reference reads "one who argues." In other
words, there is no one to argue the case for both sides.

The following translation is enlightening:

JOB 9:32,33 *(Amplified)*
**32 For [God] is not a mere man, as I am, that I should
answer Him, that we should come together in court.
33 There is no umpire between us, who might lay his
hand upon us both [would that there were]!**

Job needed one who would be able to lay his hand on him
and a hand on God. He needed one to stand between him and
God and plead his case.

— Reidt

God saw that there was no intercessor.

ISAIAH 59:16
**16 And he saw that there was no man, and wondered
that there was no intercessor: therefore his arm
brought salvation unto him; and his righteousness, it
sustained him.**

21

God saw there was no intercessor, so He supplied
the need. He sent Jesus.

Jesus, Our Intercessor

Jesus came to bridge the gap between God and sinful
man. Man needed someone to stand in the gap so he could get
back to God. Man needed an Intercessor. Jesus' sacrifice
established Him as the only fully trustworthy Intercessor for
mankind. He is the only Intercessor for the people of this
planet.

— Reidt

1 TIMOTHY 2:5
**5   For there is one God, and ONE MEDIATOR
BETWEEN GOD AND MEN, the man Christ Jesus.**

He entered Heaven to appear in the presence of God for us.
— Reidt

HEBREWS 9:24
**24 For Christ is not entered into the holy places made
with hands, which are the figures of the true; but into
heaven itself, now to appear in the presence of God
FOR US.**

He is our Intercessor at the right hand of the Father.
— Reidt

ROMANS 8:34
**34 Who is he that condemneth? It is Christ that died,
yea rather, that is risen again, who is even at the right
hand of God, WHO ALSO MAKETH INTERCESSION
FOR US.**

He saves to the uttermost. His divine power can never
cease for one moment.
— Reidt

HEBREWS 7:25
25 Wherefore he is able also to save them to the utter-
most that come unto God by him, SEEING HE EVER
LIVETH TO MAKE INTERCESSION FOR THEM.

There flows from Jesus to the Father an unceasing stream
of prayer and love for all people and for those that have
accepted Him as Savior and Lord.

Conversely there flows from the Father to Jesus the
answer for us. Therefore there flows from Jesus to every member of His Body abundant grace for every timely need.

He abideth forever. Regardless of circumstances, regardless of how dark things look, regardless of how we feel, He
abides in us forever if we continue in His goodness (Rom.
11:22).

He is our High Priest forever at the right hand of the
Father.

— Reidt

HEBREWS 7:16,17
16 Who is made, not after the law of a carnal command-
ment, but after the power of an endless life.
17 For he testifieth, Thou art a priest for ever after the
order of Melchisedec.

How long is Jesus Christ our High Priest? Forever!

HEBREWS 8:1
1 Now of the things which we have spoken this is the
sum: We have such an high priest, who is set on the
right hand of the throne of the Majesty in the heavens.

As our High Priest He exercises every function of His
office in endless Life-Power. This endless Life-Power never
ceases for one moment. Our faith and experience of that intercession need never fail because its flow is endless.

— Reidt

1 JOHN 2:1
1   My little children, these things write I unto you,
that ye sin not. And if any man sin, we have an advo-
cate with the Father, Jesus Christ the righteous.

Included in the idea of intercession is the fact that Jesus is
our Advocate. Advocate means "intercessor, consoler."

— Reidt

W. E. Vine's Expository Dictionary of New Testament Words says of the Greek word PARAKLETOS translated "advocate" in First John 2:1, "It was used in a court of justice to denote a legal assistant, counsel for the defence, an advocate; then, generally, one who pleads another's cause, an intercessor, advocate. In the widest sense, it signifies a succourer, comforter."

When a person (Christian) sins, Jesus intercedes, and
then consoles in the fact that the sin is forgiven and that the
sin and its stain is washed away by His blood leaving the person pure and clean. However, it is the will of God that a person stop sinning (1 John 2:1; 5:3).

— Reidt

First John 2:1 is not written to encourage us to sin. God wants us to stop sinning. But thank God, He did not stop with saying, *"My little children, these things write I unto you, that ye sin not. . . ."* If He had, then when we failed, we'd think, *We're out now; that's the end of it.*

No, that's just half that verse. He goes on to say, *". . . And if any man sin, we have an advocate with the Father, Jesus Christ the righteous."*

We have an Intercessor! We have a Consoler!

1 JOHN 5:3
3   For this is the love of God, that we keep his commandments: and his commandments are not grievous.

The love law of the family of God is, *"A new commandment I give unto you, That ye love one another; as I have loved you, that ye also love one another"* (John 13:34).

Every step outside of love is sin.

We tend to get our minds on dos and don'ts, but many Christians who abide perfectly by dos and don'ts are still sinning. How? By not walking in love.

Their attitudes are wrong. You need to maintain a love attitude toward your fellow man. If you do not, you are sinning.

Thank God for His intercession. Thank God for His standing in that place today to minister for us.

> Jesus spent about 3½ years in teaching and training His apostles. Since His ascension He has been interceding for about 2,000 years for the people of this earth. What a dignity this adds to prayer.
>
> — Reidt

Jesus has been interceding 2,000 years *for the people of this earth* — not just for the Church!

Notice Hebrews 7:25 again, *"Wherefore he is able also to save them to the uttermost THAT COME UNTO GOD* [This is talking about people coming unto God.] *by him, seeing he ever liveth to make intercession for them."*

Jesus' intercessory ministry includes His being our Mediator, our High Priest, our Advocate, our Consoler, and the One who prays for us at the Father's right hand.

Chapter 6
The Prayer Life of the Believer

*I exhort therefore, that, first of all, supplica-
tions, prayers, intercessions, and giving of thanks,
be made for all men; For kings, and for all that are
in authority; that we may lead a quiet and peaceable life in all godliness and honesty.*

— 1 Timothy 2:1,2

The Spirit of God, through the Apostle Paul, exhorted
believers to put something first in their prayer lives —
not second, nor third, but first.

First of all, supplications (petitions), prayers, intercessions, and giving of thanks (gratitude; grateful language to God as an act of worship), are to be made for all
men; for kings (or presidents), and for all who are in
authority.

On what grounds can we do this?

On what basis can we petition, pray, intercede, and
give thanks for others?

We can legally do it because *we are one with Jesus the
Great Intercessor, and prayer is part of His intercessory
ministry.*

One With the Great Intercessor

We have already talked about Jesus as Intercessor —
and now we see that because we are one with Him, we
are one with the Great Intercessor.

1 CORINTHIANS 6:17
17 But he that is joined unto the Lord is one spirit.

EPHESIANS 5:30
30 For we are members of his body, of his flesh, and of his bones.

2 PETER 1:4
4   Whereby are given unto us exceeding great and precious promises: that by these ye might be partakers of the divine nature, having escaped the corruption that is in the world through lust.

1 CORINTHIANS 12:27
27 Now ye are the body of Christ, and members in particular.

Christ is the Head. We are the Body. The head and the body are one. We are one with Him in carrying out His work in the earth.

He is the Great Intercessor. Therefore we are one with Him in His intercessory ministry, which includes prayer.

We are one with Him in His ministry of reconciliation.

2 CORINTHIANS 5:18-20
18 And all things are of God, who hath reconciled us to himself by Jesus Christ, and hath given to us the ministry of reconciliation;
19 To wit, that God was in Christ, reconciling the world unto himself, not imputing their trespasses unto them; and hath committed unto us the word of reconciliation.
20 Now then we are ambassadors for Christ, as though God did beseech you by us: we pray you in Christ's stead, be ye reconciled to God.

Wilford Reidt capsules it like this: "He is our great
Intercessor. He is the great Intercessor for all mankind.
As members of His Body, the Church, we partake in that
intercession."

Therefore, our prayer life will find its pattern in Him.

Identification

We must identify with the one for whom we are interceding.

Jesus identified with Mary and Martha in the death of
Lazarus. They were groaning and weeping. He groaned within
and wept. He went to the grave and raised Lazarus from the
dead.

Romans 12:15 brings in focus the idea of identification
with others: *"Rejoice with them that do rejoice, and weep with
them that weep."* The real believer can go from the house of
rejoicing . . . to the house of weeping and weep with them.

Paul identified with the Jews that he might gain the Jews.
Paul identified to them without law as without law (being not
without law to God, but under law to Christ) that he might
gain them that are without law. To the weak he became as
weak that he might gain the weak. He said that he was made
all things to all men, that he by all means might save some
(1 Cor. 9:19-22).

— Reidt

The identification we are speaking of is that identification with the object that brings deliverance.

Jesus Christ, the great Intercessor, is our Example.
He identified with man when He, who had always
existed in the form of God, emptied Himself and took the
form of a bond servant, " . . . *and was made in the like-
ness of men: And being found in fashion as a man, he
humbled himself, and became obedient unto death, even*

the death of the cross" (Phil. 2:7,8).

Jesus Christ identified with fallen man to bring our deliverance.

Through love and compassion, we also identify with those for whom we pray.

Chapter 7
Love: The Foundation For Successful Prayer

Love — the God-kind of love, "agape" — is the first prerequisite for a successful prayer life. And if you are a child of God, you have this kind of love.

ROMANS 5:5
5 . . . the love [agape] of God is shed abroad in our hearts by the Holy Ghost which is given unto us.

When you were born again, God became your Father. He is a love God. You are a love child of a love God. You are born of God, and God is love, so you are born of love. The nature of God is in you. And the nature of God is love.

Ours is a love family. Everyone in the family has God's love shed abroad in his heart, or else they are not in the family.

Now they may not be exercising it. They may be like the one-talent guy who wrapped his talent in a napkin and buried it. But the Bible declares that the love of God has been shed abroad in our hearts by the Holy Ghost. That means the God-kind of love has been shed abroad in our spirits.

This is a love family. Love is the basis for all the activity of the Body of Christ in the earth.

1 THESSALONIANS 4:9
9 But as touching brotherly love ye need not that I write unto you: for ye yourselves are taught of God to

love one another.

The love law of the family of God is:

JOHN 13:34
**34 A new commandment I give unto you, That ye love
one another; as I have loved you, that ye also love one
another.**

We are also commanded to love our enemies:

MATTHEW 5:44,45
**44 But I say unto you, Love your enemies, bless them
that curse you, do good to them that hate you, and pray
for them which despitefully use you, and persecute
you;**
**45 That ye may be the children of your Father which is
in heaven: for he maketh his sun to rise on the evil and
on the good, and sendeth rain on the just and on the
unjust.**

The reason we can do this — love our enemies, bless
them that curse us, do good to them that hate us, and
pray for them which despitefully use us and persecute
us — is because of the manner of love the Father has
bestowed upon us:

1 JOHN 3:1
**1   Behold, what manner of love the Father hath
bestowed upon us, that we should be called the sons of
God. . . .**

Your Will and Love

This *agape* love — this God-kind of love — involves
the choice of your will.

That love is inside your spirit if you are born again. But you are the one who has to will to put it into practice. You choose to let that love loose from within you.

We can choose to love all people — even our enemies. Almost anyone can love those who love them, but the Bible tells us to love our enemies.

> We choose to love all people, even the unlovable. We love as God loves. It involves (the) giving of our lives for the benefit of mankind. This does not merely refer to dying physically. It mainly refers to our being willing to give up our own will and way and take time to pray and intercede for all men.
>
> — Reidt

JOHN 15:13
13 Greater love hath no man than this, that a man lay down his life for his friends.

God loved us while we were yet sinners and sent Christ to die for us. We are to love the same way. We give our lives for mankind.

One of the ways we give our lives for mankind is by giving ourselves to prayer.

It involves sacrifice. It involves laying down our own desires for the benefit of mankind.

There is sacrifice in giving up your own will and time to pray for others.

Compassion

> Love is the basis for all Christian activity. Compassion is an ingredient of divine love.
>
> — Reidt

How do we know this is so?

Because God so loved the world that He gave Jesus.
And Jesus so loved us that He gave Himself for us. And in
His earthly ministry, again and again we see compassion.

As we look at that wonderful truth, remember that
Jesus said, *". . . he that hath seen me hath seen the
Father . . ."* (John 14:9). If you want to see God, look at
Jesus. Jesus is the will of God in action. Jesus is the love
of God in action. And in His earthly ministry, He was
moved with compassion.

> **MATTHEW 9:36-38**
> **36 But when he saw the multitudes, he was moved
> with compassion on them, because they fainted, and
> were scattered abroad, as sheep having no shepherd.
> 37 Then saith he unto his disciples, The harvest truly
> is plenteous, but the labourers are few.
> 38 Pray ye therefore the Lord of the harvest, that he
> will send forth labourers into his harvest.**

> Jesus had compassion on the people and asked us to share
> in that compassion by praying that the Lord of the Harvest
> would send laborers into the field.
>
> — Reidt

Jesus was moved with compassion and healed the
sick:

> **MATTHEW 14:14**
> **14 And Jesus went forth, and saw a great multitude,
> and was moved with compassion toward them, and he
> healed their sick.**

Jesus' compassion led to the feeding of the four thousand:

MATTHEW 15:32
32 Then Jesus called his disciples unto him, and said, I
have compassion on the multitude, because they continue with me now three days, and have nothing to eat:
and I will not send them away fasting, lest they faint in
the way.

In His compassion, Jesus healed the blind:

MATTHEW 20:34
34 So Jesus had compassion on them, and touched
their eyes: and immediately their eyes received sight,
and they followed him.

Compassion led to the healing of the leper:

MARK 1:40,41
40 And there came a leper to him, beseeching him, and
kneeling down to him, and saying unto him, If thou
wilt, thou canst make me clean.
41 And Jesus, moved with compassion, put forth his
hand, and touched him, and saith unto him, I will; be
thou clean.

In His compassion, Jesus healed every person who asked
(Matt. 4:23,24; Mark 6:56; Luke 6:19).

Jesus taught His disciples to share in His compassion by
sending out the twelve (Luke 9:1-6) and the seventy (Luke
10:1-19).

His compassion was to be carried on after His Ascension
as He made healing one of the signs of the believer (Mark
16:16-18).

His compassion was demonstrated after His Ascension
(Acts 5:15,16; 19:11,12; 28:8,9).

In every instance where Jesus was moved with compassion, the person or persons were delivered.

Human sympathy says, "I know how you feel; I'm so
sorry."

Divine compassion says, "I feel how you feel." And it brings deliverance.

Jesus felt as Mary and Martha felt as He groaned within and also wept.

— Reidt

JOHN 11:33,35
33 When Jesus therefore saw her weeping, and the Jews also weeping which came with her, he groaned in the spirit, and was troubled. . . .
35 Jesus wept.

Jesus' compassion brought deliverance. If we have the divine compassion of Jesus, there will be deliverance. But I think too much of the time we've tried to bring deliverance without God's divine compassion. That's where prayer and intercession come in.

Weeping by the unction of the Holy Spirit with them that weep brings deliverance (Rom. 12:15).

Dr. John G. Lake is known for his ministry that was well marked with apostolic ideals. He did an amazing work in South Africa just after the turn of the century.

So many healings took place in his tabernacle in Johannesburg, report of them reached the leaders of the nation. Some of the top government people sought him for help on the behalf of the wife of a certain government official.

When Lake went to her home, he found her bedridden with terminal cancer. He determined that she was a Christian. Then he began to give her Scripture to teach her about divine healing and to get her faith activated.

She made a decision to trust God for her healing. The doctors had given her up to die and were only giving her pain relievers to keep her comfortable. But she decided to stop all drugs.

She said, "If I'm going to trust God for my healing, and I am, then I'm going to throw myself completely over on His mercy."

"This woman was in such pain," Lake said, "that one of the ministers of the church and I stayed at her bedside around the clock, praying. As we prayed, she would get relief."

One morning, after having prayed all night, Lake went home just long enough to bathe and shave. Then he started back.

"When I came within two blocks of the house," Lake said, "I heard the woman screaming in pain. At the sound of those screams, somehow I seemed to enter into a divine compassion. . . ."

Lake entered into the sufferings of Jesus. He began to feel just like Jesus feels. For Jesus can be touched with the feelings of our infirmities (Heb. 4:15).

Lake said, "I found myself running those last two blocks without even thinking what I was doing. Without thinking, I rushed into the room, sat down on the edge of the bed, picked up that emaciated body in my arms like a baby, and began to weep. While I was weeping, she was perfectly healed."

Somehow, the compassion of Jesus, the love of God, was able to permeate his heart, his spirit.

Dedicated believers can enter into that area of compassion by one way — and you will not get there any other way — and it is by fellowship with God.

You cannot fellowship with God, you cannot sit in the

Presence of the Great God of this universe without His love permeating your being, and without His compassion flowing into you.

And it is when you can get into this place that you will be able to do as Jesus said in John chapter 14.

JOHN 14:12
12 Verily, verily, I say unto you, He that believeth on me, the works that I do shall he do also; and greater works than these shall he do; because I go unto my Father.

The works that He did were born out of love and compassion. The works that the believing ones shall do, including prayer, are products of sharing in His ministry of love and compassion.

Chapter 8
Knowing God's Love

And to know the love of Christ, which passeth knowledge, that ye might be filled with all the fulness of God.

— Ephesians 3:19

To intercede effectively, you must know the great love God has for all humanity.

He sends the rain on the just and the unjust (Matt. 5:45).
He makes the sun to rise on the evil and the good (Matt. 5:45).
He is kind to the unthankful and to the evil (Luke 6:35).

— Reidt

Since the love of God is in us, and the love of God has been shed abroad in our hearts, we are to be kind like God is kind — to the unthankful and to the evil.

Whosoever Will

Jesus purchased a gift of salvation for anyone who would accept it (Eph. 2:8; Rev. 22:17). God commands all men everywhere to repent (Acts 17:30). His hand of mercy is extended to all mankind.

Our intercession for all men is not so much for God to extend His mercy. This He has already done through Jesus.

Our intercession is mainly to break the bondage that the devil has over men.

The devil has blinded men (2 Cor. 4:3,4). We are to loose the sinner from the blindness that he may see the Light.

— Reidt

One afternoon a number of years ago, I was lying across my bed resting between the morning and evening service. I had my Bible and another book and I was studying. Into my spirit — not into my mind — came an understanding of some of these things I'd never had before. I saw this scripture in a way I'd never seen it up to that time:

2 CORINTHIANS 4:3,4
3   But if our gospel be hid, it is hid to them that are lost:
4   In whom the god of this world hath blinded the minds of them which believe not, lest the light of the glorious gospel of Christ, who is the image of God, should shine unto them.

I saw how we had missed it in praying for the lost.

I don't mean it unkindly, but just to say, "God save Uncle John and Aunt Lucy," does about as much good as it does to twiddle your thumbs and say, "Twinkle, twinkle, little star." God has already done all He's going to do about saving them.

But I didn't know that — until that afternoon. I'd been praying like that about my own relatives.

That afternoon, I heard the Lord say to my spirit, "No human in his right mind would drive his car down the highway 100 miles an hour, past blinking red warning lights, past signs that said, 'Danger! Bridge out!' and plunge himself out into eternity. But a drunk man would — a doped man would. The same thing is true spiritually. No man in his right mind would plunge himself out into eternity without God. But the god of this world has blinded their minds."

He gave me this scripture, *"In whom the god of this*

world hath blinded the minds . . ." (2 Cor. 4:4).

I could hear the Spirit of God challenging me, "You've approached it wrongly. You've worked on the wrong end of the thing. You've fasted and prayed that I would do something and I've done all I'm ever going to do. The blood has already been shed. The Gospel has already been given. The light is already here. It can't shine in because of what the devil has done. What you've got to do is break the power of the devil over them."

Intercession does not change God — God never changes.

Prayer does not change God. Prayer changes you and it changes others. It does not change God.

I saw what I had to do for my brother, Dub. I'd been fasting and praying that God would save him off and on for 15 years, and if it ever did any good, I couldn't tell it. Dub was the black sheep of the family. Anything you could mention, he'd done. I knew if breaking the power of the devil would work on him, it would work on anyone.

I rose up off the bed with my Bible in one hand, and the other hand lifted, saying, "In the Name of the Lord Jesus Christ, I break the power of the devil over my brother Dub's life, and I claim his deliverance. (That meant I claimed his deliverance from that blindness, that bondage of Satan.) And I claim his full salvation in the Name of the Lord Jesus Christ."

Within three weeks, my brother was born again.

Here is where intercession comes in — we are to loose the sinner from the blindness that he may see the light.

If we can get people to see God as He really is, they'll

want to love Him.

We are one with the great Intercessor in His ministry of reconciliation.

Let's look at this Scripture again in the *Amplified* translation:

2 CORINTHIANS 5:19 *(Amplified)*
19 It was God (personally present) in Christ, reconciling and restoring the world to favor with Himself, not counting up and holding against [men] their trespasses [but cancelling them]; and committing to us the message of reconciliation — of the restoration to favor.

Whom did He reconcile unto Himself? The world!

Whose trespasses are canceled? The world's!

That's what will be so terrible — people will go to hell, and when they get there, they'll find out we hadn't told them the truth. We hadn't told them everything was canceled out.

The sins of the unsaved have been canceled out by Jesus. That's how God is kind to the unthankful and the evil. And He has given to us that message, that word of reconciliation.

Yet we have preached, "God is going to get you if you don't watch out. He's after you."

People have trained their children, saying, "Don't do that. Jesus won't love you if you do that."

That's a lie. He may not want them to do it, but He'll still love them anyhow.

Telling children, "God won't love you, if you do that," causes them to grow up with their minds blinded to the light of His love. And it's very difficult to get that kind of teaching out of people.

He has given to us the ministry of reconciliation.

We used to think we had to preach people under conviction. So we went out and beat them over the head, so to speak.

No! The Spirit of God will convict them.

Ours is the ministry of reconciliation. When we can get people to see God as He really is, they will want to love Him.

Chapter 9
Boldness

Let us therefore come BOLDLY unto the throne of grace, that we may obtain mercy, and find grace to help in time of need.

— Hebrews 4:16

Effective prayer involves boldness.
We come before God's throne with boldness.
Where do we get boldness? In Jesus!

EPHESIANS 3:11,12
11 According to the eternal purpose which he purposed in Christ Jesus our Lord:
12 In whom we have boldness and access with confidence by the faith of him.

There are many things you do not need to pray for — but it is all right to pray for boldness. You should, in fact.

For example, you do not need to pray for faith. The Bible says, "*. . . faith cometh by hearing, and hearing by the word of God*" (Rom. 10:17).

So you know how to get faith. Faith is increased by feeding it on God's Word and by exercising it. We do not need to pray for faith. But the Bible does show us that we can pray for boldness.

Peter and John were bold when they used the Name of Jesus to minister to the lame man at the gate called Beautiful. They were bold when they proclaimed the Name of Jesus to the crowd that gathered.

The Jewish authorities noticed their boldness and took them in for questioning (Acts 4:13). They commanded them to preach and teach no more in the Name of Jesus.

Being let go, they went to their own company and reported all the chief priests and elders had said to them. Then the whole company of believers lifted up their voice with one accord in prayer unto God.

ACTS 4:29,30
29 And now, Lord, behold their threatenings: and grant unto thy servants, that WITH ALL BOLDNESS they may speak thy word,
30 By stretching forth thine hand to heal; and that signs and wonders may be done by the name of thy holy child Jesus.

That prayer was answered!

ACTS 4:31
31 And when they had prayed, the place was shaken where they were assembled together; and they were all filled with the Holy Ghost, and they spake the word of God with BOLDNESS.

Paul asked the church at Ephesus to pray for him. This great man of God, this apostle of faith, this man who wrote half the New Testament, said, *"Praying always . . . for all saints; And for me, that utterance may be given unto me, that I may open my mouth BOLDLY, to make known the mystery of the gospel, For which I am an ambassador in bonds: that therein I may speak BOLDLY, as I ought to speak"* (Eph. 6:18-21).

The Ephesians' prayer for Paul was a prayer of supplication.

Boldness To Act

We need boldness to act. Sometimes during intercession the Holy Spirit may bid us to go to the one we are interceding for. I now refer to an incident in the life of a great intercessor, Charlie Hollandsworth of Spokane. One day he entered into intercession for someone. He did not know for whom he was interceding. After a time of agonizing in the Spirit he was bidden of the Spirit to go to the Monroe Street Bridge. He hurried to the bridge without delay. As he arrived, in the middle of the bridge the Holy Spirit pointed out a man with one leg over the railing ready to jump to his death. Charlie stopped the car quickly and grabbed the man. He persuaded the man to get into his car.

He drove the man out into the country where they could be alone. It took between two and three hours to get the man to accept the Lord Jesus as His Saviour.

— Reidt

We may not know for what to pray, but thank God, the Holy Spirit does. We need boldness to act on God's Word. We need boldness to act on what the Spirit of God may say to us.

I can sense the Spirit of God searching through the Church trying to find those whom He can trust to pray and to act with boldness. He needs them.

Many people have jobs and duties which do not allow them to give themselves wholeheartedly to intercession. Yet I have found that as you go about doing whatever you have to do, on the inside of you, you can be praying.

God will not lay a burden of intercession upon you unless you are available to move. He might move on you to pray for someone while you are working if the work is such that you can pray.

— Reidt

There are jobs where it would be very difficult for you to pray while working. So God would have to seek out someone else.

But there are some jobs — particularly if you are not working with your mind, but with your hands — where you could give yourself to prayer even while you're working.

Don't throw off that burden to pray when it comes. Be bold to act on it.

One day while I was still pastoring, I was driving along attending to some business and visiting people. Suddenly, I had an urge to pray for my younger brother. He was backslidden at the time and was not walking with the Lord. An alarm went off within me.

So I went along praying on the inside of me, even while I was talking to other people — on the inside of me something was reaching out to God on his behalf.

I carried that thing around with me two or three days until it just lifted. I didn't know what it concerned.

Later on, in conversation, my brother said to me, "I'll tell you one thing, the Lord sure helped me the other day."

At the time, he was a businessman, and he owned a ranch. He told me that he was out on the ranch when a 5-gallon can of gasoline he was holding in his hand exploded. He was not the least bit hurt.

He said everyone who saw it was amazed.

The ranch manager said, "That beats anything I ever saw in my life. I can't believe what I saw."

But three days before it happened, I was praying. I am satisfied if I had thrown that off and not yielded to it, he could have been severely burned and perhaps killed.

You see, God didn't want him to leave here in that backslidden condition.

What if I hadn't prayed?

What if Charlie Hollandsworth hadn't been responsive to the Spirit of God? What if he hadn't interceded when he didn't know who he was interceding for? What if he had been too busy, or unresponsive to the leading of the Spirit to rush out to that bridge not even knowing why he was going?

In all probability, that man would have gone to hell.

It's a sobering thought that when men come before the judgment bar of God, there may be some people in hell who will point to us and say, "You are responsible."

Boldness Before the Throne

ISAIAH 43:25,26
25 I, even I, am he that blotteth out thy transgressions for mine own sake, and will not remember thy sins.
26 Put me in remembrance: let us plead together: declare thou, that thou mayest be justified.

Here is a challenge from the covenant-keeping God to Israel. It is also a challenge to the Church. For if God kept His covenant with them, He will keep His covenant with us.

The believer has covenant rights in prayer, as well as other covenant rights.

Yet there is one outstanding problem that defeats believers in their prayer life. When we come to God, we have a feeling of inferiority, a sense of sin-consciousness, because we know we have failed. We have a guilt complex.

Some begin their prayers with, "I'm so weak and

unworthy," and then harp on their weakness and unworthiness throughout the prayer.

And when they come into the presence of God telling Him that, they talk themselves out of faith and into condemnation. They don't know whether God hears them or not. All they do is beg for crumbs.

But look at what God said. *"I, even I, am he that blotteth out thy transgressions for mine own sake, and will not remember thy sins"* (Isa. 43:25).

Why did he say He would blot out our transgressions? For His own sake — so He could bless us. He couldn't have blessed us without it.

When we know that He blotted out our sin, that He doesn't even remember that we ever did anything wrong, we can come to Him with confidence. We can come with faith. We lose sin-consciousness — and now we have Son-consciousness!

We don't have to sit on a curbstone out in front of our mansion, begging for favors. We can come in boldly through the front door and enter the throne room to fellowship with God.

We are sons of God. We are joint-heirs with Jesus Christ. We are covenant people. We have a legal right. A gospel right. A son right. A family right. A Body right to enter the throne room.

When Jesus went into the presence of the Father, He didn't go in with just His head, leaving His little finger outside saying, "Oh, I'm embarrassed." No! He didn't have any condemnation even in His little finger.

We are the Body of Christ. That means the Body can go into the Presence of God the Father with the same confidence and assurance that the Head can! *Boldly!*

Chapter 10
Elements of the Believer's Prayer Life

Let's look at the elements of an effective prayer life.

Fervency

JAMES 5:16-18 *(Worrell)*
16 ... A righteous man's inwrought supplication avails much.
17 Elijah was a man of like nature with us; and he prayed earnestly that it might not rain, and it rained not on the earth for three years and six months;
18 And again he prayed, and the heaven gave rain, and the earth brought forth its fruit.

Effective prayer involves fervency.

The Bible teaches that we are always to be ". . . *fervent in spirit . . .*" (Rom. 12:11).

W. E. Vine says the word translated "fervent" in Romans 12:11 means *to be hot; to boil. Strong's Exhaustive Concordance of the Bible* adds that figuratively it means to be earnest.

Epaphrus was "laboring fervently" for the Colossians in prayers (Col. 4:12). The Greek word *agonizomai,* translated "laboring fervently," indicates a striving, a wrestling.

Desire

2 CORINTHIANS 7:6,7
6 ... God ... comforted us by the coming of Titus;

**7   And not by his coming only, but by the consolation
wherewith he was comforted in you, when he told us
your EARNEST DESIRE, your mourning, your FER-
VENT mind toward me; so that I rejoiced the more.**

The Corinthians' "earnest desire" was recognized by Titus
and conveyed to Paul.

Something happens when the real God-cry, the real God-
prayer, and the real God-yearning gets ahold of our spirit.

God lays it on your heart to intercede, then this [burden,
or whatever it is God has laid on your heart] should be the
paramount issue of your heart.

When the desire to see the answer come is intensified so
that it absorbs all the energies, then the time for the fulfill-
ment is not far away.

This is the desire that brings the answer. It is creative
desire.

— Reidt

In the winter of 1942 and 1943, I found myself taken
up with a desire for God to move. I did not conjure it
up — it was put there, no doubt, by God.

You see, what is happening in the move of the Spirit
of God — revivals and so forth — doesn't come as the
result of somebody's praying yesterday or even last
week. It is the result of the prayers of yesteryear.

That winter of '42 and '43 I was pastor of a church in
East Texas when I found myself so taken up, and so burdened, praying along certain lines.

During those war years it seemed as though many of
our churches dried up. People were busy going to war, or
working in war plants, and so forth. In our Pentecostal
churches we had an abundance of tongues and interpre-
tations, but seldom, if ever, did we see any other gifts or

manifestations of the Spirit.

I found myself almost unconsciously praying, "Dear Lord, may the more mighty gifts and manifestations of the Spirit come into manifestation and operation . . . the gift of special faith . . . the working of miracles . . . the gifts of healings. . . ."

I was so taken up with that, I would wake up in the living room on my knees at 3 or 4 o'clock in the morning praying that. Night after night, it was a common occurrence. Many times I would have been awakened earlier in the night. I'd get out of the bedroom so I wouldn't disturb my wife. (I do a lot of praying quietly and privately, but I couldn't be quiet about this. It seemed as if I were going to burst.) But other times, I wouldn't remember getting up. I would find myself out in the living room praying and say to myself, *How did I get here?*

Many times I would awaken and find myself unconsciously praying, "May these greater, more mighty manifestations of your Spirit come into operation. . . ."

Then on the 23rd day of February 1943, after praying that day for 5 hours and 45 minutes, God began to say something to me. I got my pencil and wrote it down. He said, "At the close of World War II, there will come a revival of divine healing to America."

That was more than two years before the war was over. The war wasn't over until August 1945; this happened in 1943.

Nineteen months later, in September 1944, I was speaking at a Christ's Ambassadors Rally for the Assemblies of God. I started out on another subject, but because this was burning inside me, I got over on this subject and told what the Lord had said to me.

I said, "I want to give you a preview of what is going to happen when the war is over. There is coming a revival of divine healing to America."

When I said that, the power of God fell on that crowd. Every minister, just like somebody told them to (and I did not), got up and ran to the altar. Every person hit the floor. I had never seen such a sight in my life.

Thank God for the Spirit of God. Thank God for prayer.

That revival of divine healing came. It started in 1947. But it didn't come because somebody had prayed the week before in 1947. It came because people — not just me, but others — were praying back in 1943.

When I was praying about it, it was a consuming desire. I did not care or even suspect that God would use me in it. I didn't really even want Him to use me. It would suit me just fine if I was behind the scenes where I could pray and nobody ever saw me.

God carries out His will upon the earth through the Church.

What if people had not responded to that burden?

Where did it come from, anyhow? Did we conjure it up ourselves? No! God laid it on our hearts. It was a consuming desire.

What if we hadn't responded? We didn't have to. We're not robots.

God doesn't *make* us do anything. We have a will of our own. We have to will to respond to the Spirit of God. God's Spirit doesn't use force. If He did, He'd make everybody get saved today and we'd go into the Millennium tomorrow.

It is the devil and demons that drive and force people.

The Holy Spirit leads and guides; He will give a gentle push.

Be determined to respond to the Spirit of God. Respond to those *urges* to pray. Sometimes there is a *leading;* sometimes there is a *burden.*

Become sensitive to Him.

Sometimes we're insensitive to what He's saying in our spirits, because we live too much in the mental realm. And we pass by these things.

> Some may object to having something become the supreme desire of the heart for a time. They say your supreme desire should be for the Lord.
>
> — Reidt

When God lays that desire on your heart, that is your supreme desire for the Lord. God dwells in you. And He is the One who activates the desire. It is God's supreme desire for people to be delivered.

It was God's supreme desire that that man (in Chapter 9) not jump off the bridge and commit suicide. The man happened to be where God could find someone to start praying — someone close enough to respond to the Spirit of God and get in his car and drive out there. The man's life was saved and he was born again, because a child of God let God's supreme desire become his supreme desire.

> God is not halfhearted about anything. Since it is His supreme desire, it also becomes the supreme desire of the one called on to intercede. It is cooperation with God. "For we are labourers together with God . . ." (1 Cor. 3:9).
>
> — Reidt

Perseverance

EPHESIANS 6:18
**18 Praying always with all prayer and supplication in
the Spirit, and watching thereunto with all perseverance and supplication for all saints.**

Effective prayer must include the element of perseverance. Wilford Reidt sums it up well:

> When the Holy Spirit lays it upon a person's heart to
> intercede, the intercession should not stop until the answer is
> given or the burden lifted. In my experience where for the
> most part I do not know for whom I am interceding, I have
> had burdens last for hours and even days. I had to do usual
> work, but all the time there was that inner groaning in my
> spirit. The times when I had opportunity to get alone with
> God, the burden intensified. There is no rule to follow. Each
> person will do as God directs.
>
> The reason "persistence" is an ingredient of intercession is
> that it is easy to throw off a burden and forget it. It is an awe-
> some responsibility to feel that someone's life may depend on
> your intercession. Not many believers are willing to accept it.
> So those that are willing are usually kept very busy.

Fasting

1 SAMUEL 10:7
**7   And let it be, when these signs are come unto thee,
that thou do as occasion serve thee; for God is with
thee.**

Effective prayer sometimes involves fasting.

> In some cases fasting may be necessary. There is no hard
> and fast rule. The prayer warrior will do as occasion shall
> serve him. If he deems fasting necessary, then fast.
>
> — Reidt

In all the epistles — the books of the New Testament written to the Church — not one time do they tell the Church to fast.

That doesn't mean we should not. Mention is made of fasting, but no rules are laid down, nor do they even encourage the Church to fast.

The reason is, there are no hard and fast rules about it — it is to be done as the occasion arises.

Fasting does not change God. He is the same before you fast, while you are fasting, and when you get through fasting.

But fasting will change you. It will help you keep the flesh under. It will help you become more susceptible to the Spirit of God.

The Lord may speak to you to fast. He has spoken to me to fast at special times. I might mention, however, that never have I been led to fast more than three days at a time. (For more information on this subject, *see* Brother Hagin's book, *A Commonsense Guide to Fasting*.)

Chapter 11
The Holy Spirit: Our Helper in Prayer

The Holy Spirit intercedes for us.
The Holy Spirit also *helps* us to pray.

ROMANS 8:26,27
**26 Likewise the Spirit also HELPETH our infirmities:
for we know not what we should pray for as we ought:
but the Spirit itself [Himself] maketh intercession for us
with groanings which cannot be uttered.
27 And he that searcheth the hearts knoweth what is
the mind of the Spirit, because he maketh intercession
for the saints according to the will of God.**

Dr. T. J. McCrossan, who was a noted professor of
Greek, included this enlightening insight into the Greek
word translated "helpeth" in his book, *Bodily Healing
and the Atonement* (now available from Kenneth Hagin's
Faith Library):

> ... note well the word here translated "helpeth" *(sunantil-
> ambanetai).* This is the present tense, 3rd person singular of
> the deponent verb *sunantilambanomai,* and comes from *sun,*
> together with; *anti,* against; and *lambano,* I take hold of. This
> word, therefore, means "to take hold against together with."
>   Thus, in Romans 8:26 we are told that the Holy Ghost
> takes hold against our sicknesses together with someone.
> With whom? Why, with ourselves. ...
>   — McCrossan

Dr. McCrossan was dealing with only one side of infir-

mity (feebleness of body; sickness), but we can clearly
see that the Holy Spirit helps by taking hold together
with us against our infirmities or all manner of weakness.

If I said from the platform, "Some of you men stay
after the service and help us move this piano off the
platform," I would mean that I wanted them to take
hold, together with someone else, against the weight of
the piano.

The Holy Spirit helps. He takes hold together with us
against the infirmity. If we do not take hold together
with against — He has nothing to do. We must take hold
together with first — then the Holy Spirit will help us.

Someone once said to me, "Since I found out the Holy
Spirit is doing my praying for me, I don't do too much
praying anymore."

Romans 8:26 does not say that the Holy Spirit does
our praying for us. He *helps* us. If the Holy Spirit did our
praying for us, that would make Him responsible for our
prayer life, and that's out of line with the Bible.

Read what Jesus said in the Four Gospels relative to
the Holy Spirit. For instance, *"And I will pray the
Father, and he shall give you another Comforter, that he
may abide with you for ever; Even the Spirit of truth;
whom the world cannot receive, because it seeth him not,
neither knoweth him: but ye know him; for he dwelleth
with you, and shall be in you. I will not leave you com-
fortless: . . . But the Comforter, which is the Holy Ghost,
whom the Father will send in my name, he shall teach
you all things, and bring all things to your remembrance,
whatsoever I have said unto you"* (John 14:16-18,26).

The Greek word *Paraclete* here translated "Comforter" literally means *one called alongside to help.*

The *Amplified* translation gives the sevenfold meaning of the word: Comforter, Counselor, Helper, Intercessor, Advocate, Strengthener, Standby.

The Holy Spirit is not sent to do the Christians' work for them; He is sent to help them do it.

Jesus told the disciples to tarry in Jerusalem until they were baptized with the Holy Ghost. He said, ". . . *ye shall receive power, after that the Holy Ghost is come upon you: and ye shall be witnesses unto me . . .*" (Acts 1:8).

One meaning of the Greek word translated power here is "ability." Another way to say it is this, "After the Holy Spirit comes upon you, you shall receive ability." Ability to do what? To be witnesses.

Now the Holy Spirit is not going to do the witnessing — you are going to do the witnessing with His ability.

Likewise the Holy Spirit will not do your praying for you — but you are going to be able to pray with His ability. He will *help* you do it.

We're the ones who are responsible for our lives.

We're the ones who are responsible to spread the gospel.

We're the ones who are responsible to pray. The Holy Spirit is our Helper.

Chapter 12
The Holy Spirit and Our Infirmities

Likewise the Spirit also helpeth our INFIRMI-TIES. . . .

— Romans 8:26

What does the word "infirmities" mean in this setting? W. E. *Vine's Expository Dictionary of New Testament Words* defines the Greek word as: want of strength, weakness, indicating inability to produce results.

Our infirmities would keep us from producing prayer results were it not for our divine Helper, the Spirit of God.

Ignorance

"Ignorance is an infirmity," Reidt points out. "We do not always *know."*

The enemy will take advantage of us in areas of ignorance. God says, *"My people are destroyed for lack of knowledge . . ."* (Hosea 4:6). Also, it is impossible for us to pray with accuracy when we don't know for what to pray. That is why we need the Holy Spirit to "help" us in this infirmity. Paul prayed for the Colossians that they would *know.* (And in his prayer we find a clue as to how to pray for fellow Christians.)

COLOSSIANS 1:9
9 For this cause we also, since the day we heard it, DO NOT CEASE TO PRAY for you, and to desire that ye

MIGHT BE FILLED WITH THE KNOWLEDGE OF HIS WILL IN ALL WISDOM AND SPIRITUAL UNDERSTANDING.

The will of God and the Word of God are connected.

God has given us His written Word to reveal to us His will. We are to renew our minds with His Word so that the first thing which comes to mind in a given situation is what God has to say on the subject.

ROMANS 12:2
2   And be not conformed to this world: but be ye transformed by the renewing of your mind, that ye may prove what is that good, and acceptable, and perfect, will of God.

God has given us His Word. The Holy Spirit takes that Word and brings it to our remembrance. Then we know the will of God if we know the Word of God.

JOHN 14:26
26 But the Comforter, which is the Holy Ghost, whom the Father will send in my name, he shall teach you all things, and bring all things to your remembrance, whatsoever I have said unto you.

Then, thanks be unto God, for things the Word does not cover, we have an unction from the Holy One.

1 JOHN 2:20
20 But ye have an unction from the Holy One, and ye know all things.

Dullness of Perception

Dullness of perception is an infirmity. Jesus referred to

this in Luke 24:25 when He said, "O fools, and slow of heart to believe all that the prophets have spoken."

— Reidt

So the church in Ephesus wouldn't be dull to perceive, Paul prayed.

EPHESIANS 1:16-18
16 [I] Cease not to give thanks for you, making mention of you in my prayers.
17 That the God of our Lord Jesus Christ, the Father of glory, MAY GIVE UNTO YOU THE SPIRIT OF WISDOM and REVELATION in the KNOWLEDGE OF HIM:
18 The EYES OF YOUR UNDERSTANDING BEING ENLIGHTENED; THAT YE MAY KNOW what is the hope of his calling, and what the riches of the glory of his inheritance in the saints.

(Again, as in his prayer for the Colossians, Paul's Spirit-anointed prayer shows us how we can pray for ourselves and for other believers to overcome dullness of perception concerning things of the Lord.)

The Holy Spirit is given to teach us all things (John 14:26). He teaches us directly in our own spirits. But He also teaches us through teachers who know the Word of God. God put teachers in the Church (Eph. 4:11,12). Do not limit the amount of knowledge you can acquire from God.

ROMANS 15:14
14 And I myself also am persuaded of you, my brethren, that ye also are full of goodness, FILLED WITH ALL KNOWLEDGE, able also to admonish one another.

That's where God wants us to be!

Chapter 13
Prayer for the Sick

Another definition of the word translated "infirmity" in Romans 8:26 is "feebleness of body; frailty; sickness."

Prayer is often necessary against this infirmity.

When I teach on faith and healing in crusades and seminars, I can only cover one side of it. The meetings are not long enough to cover the entire picture. Therefore I have one purpose in mind — to move people to believe God now and receive from God now. Thank God, a certain percentage of them can and will.

We know — because we have the Bible and the Bible imparts unto us the knowledge of God — that healing is provided for everyone. We know it is the highest and the perfect will of God that every believer not be sick, but live out his full length of time here below until his body wears out and he falls asleep in Jesus.

We've got to present God's perfect will or people won't know about it. But we also know from the natural standpoint that for a number of reasons that does not happen with everybody — even all of God's children.

(If it does not, it doesn't mean the people were not saved. It does not mean they did not go to Heaven.)

We know from the Old Testament that God made a covenant with Israel.

EXODUS 23:25,26
25 And ye shall serve the Lord your God, and he shall bless thy bread, and thy water; and I will take sickness away from the midst of thee.

26 There shall nothing cast their young, nor be barren, in thy land: the number of thy days I will fulfil.

Wasn't that God's perfect will? Yes!

But notice, it was conditional.

What was the condition? That they walk in His statutes and keep His commandments.

As long as Israel kept the covenant there was no sickness among them. No babies or young people died.

But then sickness and disease invaded them and people began dying young. Why? Because they did not keep their covenant with God.

Even in the household of King David, his child was sick and the prophet foretold the child would die (2 Sam. 12:14).

How did the prophet know that? By the Spirit of God.

It was not the perfect will of God that the child die, but through sin the covenant was broken. The Spirit of God said what would happen under the circumstances.

The same thing that happened with Israel happens with individuals today. We have to tell people what God's plan is and what God's covenant is and what belongs to them. Healing is ours. Healing is in the atonement. Yet not everyone is walking in their New Covenant rights.

Sometimes — if they are bona fide baby Christians — you can exercise your faith for them. You can carry them on your faith for a while.

Sometimes you can get them to agree with you. You can join your faith with theirs in the prayer of agreement (Matt. 18:19). It works.

But there are still those who do not know, and who do

not understand, for whom prayer must be made.

A denominational minister who still pastored his church told me that his wife had been marvelously healed by the power of God after medical science had given up on her case. Her healing brought them into the Charismatic Movement.

"After my wife was healed," he said, "we began to get our eyes opened to the baptism in the Holy Spirit." They were filled with the Holy Spirit and were relatively new in the things of the Spirit when his wife had an experience in prayer for someone else's healing.

A young wife and mother of three who attended this pastor's church regularly had to have open heart surgery. She died on the operating table. After some time she was resuscitated, but she did not regain consciousness.

The doctors said she would never regain consciousness — and that this was just as well, for her mind would never be right; she had been without oxygen to her brain for too long.

This pastor told me, "We comforted the young husband and prayed with him all we could — but we were so new in this. Yet this young man's wife persisted in living.

The pastor said, "The third night I woke up and suddenly realized my wife wasn't in bed. After a little while I got up to look for her. I heard groanings from the living room. I thought, *She got up and fell and hurt herself.* I found her lying flat on the living room floor groaning."

He got down beside her and said, "Honey, what's the matter?"

She said, "I don't know. I don't understand it, but I just can't let her die. I just can't do it."

For three nights, every night, she lay on the floor and groaned and prayed out loud all night long.

On the fourth day after the pastor's wife had prayed for three nights, suddenly, that young woman in the hospital came to herself. The doctors were amazed. Her mind was clear. She was perfectly all right. She was restored to her husband and children.

Even though this pastor's wife was new in this, she began to pray for the young woman mainly because the Spirit of God gave it to her — not because she worked it up.

How dependent we are upon the Holy Spirit in our prayer life.

In dealing with the sick, I find that sometimes the Spirit of God hooks up with me and prays through me.

And there are times I have tried to get Him to but He does not. You cannot make the Spirit of God do anything. Instead of using the Spirit, let the Spirit use you.

Thirty years ago I went to a man's bedside to pray for his healing. And I couldn't even say the word "heal." I'd say, "Oh, God," and then instead of saying the word *"heal,"* I'd say, *"bless* this man." I tried to make my tongue say "heal" and it would not. I couldn't control my tongue.

I said, "Lord, why can't I pray for this man's healing? He's not old enough to die. You promised us a minimum of 70 or 80 years."

(In Psalm 91, He actually said, "with long life will I satisfy you." If we are not satisfied at the end of 70 or 80 years, we can go on until we are satisfied.)

But the Lord said to me, "Yes, but he was born again 36 years ago. I've been waiting on him to put away sin for 36 years. [Think about the patience of God!] He's never lived right over two weeks at a time in 36 years. So I judged him and turned him over to Satan for the destruction of the flesh that his spirit may be saved in the day of the Lord Jesus."

(That's in the Bible. Read the fifth chapter of First Corinthians and the last part of the eleventh chapter.)

Then the Spirit said to me, "You can't pray for his healing, but you can do this. Tell him you are going to lay your hands on him to be filled with the Holy Spirit, and his last days will be better than his first."

I told him what the Lord said. When I laid my hand on his forehead, instantly, he started speaking with tongues.

I left and went my way. When I came back over a month later, he was dead and buried. But they told me he sat up in bed and sang and talked in tongues three days and nights. Then he had a glorious homegoing.

That wasn't God's perfect will for him. But it certainly beat going to hell.

I went off down the highway in my car, crying and singing, "Grace, grace, God's grace. Grace that is greater than all of our sins."

Sometimes I have tried to pray for people, and it would seem like I ran up against a blank wall, or down a blind alley. I just didn't get anywhere because the Spirit of God didn't take hold with me.

Identification

Sometimes in praying for others against physical sickness it will seem in the spirit — literally, physically it is not so — but it will seem in the spirit that the same thing fastens itself upon your body. You see, you are taking another's need before God.

Sometimes I hurt just like they hurt. If they are sick to their stomach, I get sick to my stomach. If they can't breathe, I gasp for breath. I am identifying with them. Of course, this is an operation of the Spirit and not something to be sought after in your prayer life. These kinds of manifestations only occur as the Holy Spirit wills — not as we will.

Since 1949, with only one exception, every time I have prayed that way for the sick and taken on their symptoms, they always received their healing. And in the case of that one exception, Jesus appeared on the scene and said, "I have come to heal him, but he won't let me."

Chapter 14
What Is Praying in the Spirit?

Since praying in the Spirit is so important, I wanted to include this chapter to explain it more fully.

Effective prayer in the Spirit can be made two ways:

1. In your own known language.

Not much has been said about praying in your known language as a form of praying in the Spirit, but it is a realm of prayer that takes a person a step beyond praying with his own understanding.

Praying in the Spirit in your known language occurs when you become more conscious of God and spiritual things than you are of your natural surroundings. The old-timers used to call it being "lost in the Spirit." During such times a person can become caught up in prayer to the extent that he can pray for two or three hours and think only ten minutes have passed.

It is also possible while praying in the Spirit in your own known language, to speak things out in prayer that would otherwise never have occurred to you. You are actually speaking under divine inspiration much like the inspiration that occurs in the gift of prophecy.

2. In other tongues.

What is praying in the Spirit?

EPHESIANS 6:18
18 Praying always with all prayer and supplication IN THE SPIRIT, and watching thereunto with all perseverance and supplication for all saints.

What does this verse mean, *"Praying . . . in the
Spirit . . ."* (Eph. 6:18)?

I faced this question many years ago as a Baptist pastor. Somehow I knew inside me that whatever it was, I
wasn't doing it.

I wanted to know. I asked everyone I could find to ask
what it meant.

Do you know what most people thought praying in
the Spirit was? They thought it was praying with just a
little more vim, vigor, and vitality!

Then, too, Jude's statement written to believers puz-
zled me.

JUDE 20
**20 But ye, beloved, building up yourselves on your
most holy faith, PRAYING IN THE HOLY GHOST.**

I asked myself, "What is praying in the Holy Ghost?"

Whatever it was, I felt I wasn't doing it.

Now my head told me I was "praying in the Spirit"
and "praying in the Holy Ghost."

But my heart told me, "You are not."

So I set out to find out for sure what those expres-
sions mean.

I thought, *Paul is doing the writing here in Ephesians
where he speaks of "praying in the Spirit." Did he ever
say anything anywhere else about praying in the Spirit?
If he did, then he is talking about the same thing, wher-
ever he speaks of it.*

So I began to run references on this phrase in Paul's
writings. They led me to the 14th chapter of First
Corinthians.

Now I hadn't gotten into the 14th chapter of First Corinthians too much. The first Sunday of each quarter, I preached from the 11th chapter just before we took the Lord's Supper. I would skip the 12th chapter and preach about love in the 13th chapter. Then I would skip over the 14th chapter and preach about the Resurrection in the 15th chapter. I was almost afraid of the 12th and 14th chapters.

But I could see that if I was going to find out about praying in the Spirit, I had to get there, because it is there that Paul said something about it. I found out what he said.

1 CORINTHIANS 14:2
2 For he that speaketh in a unknown tongue speaketh not unto men, but unto God: for no man understandeth him; howbeit IN THE SPIRIT he speaketh mysteries.

In the Spirit! In the Spirit! In the Spirit he speaketh mysteries! There it was again!

Now notice something further down in the chapter.

1 CORINTHIANS 14:14,15
14 For if I pray in an unknown tongue, my spirit prayeth, but my understanding is unfruitful.
15 What is it then? I will pray with the spirit, and I will pray with the understanding also: I will sing with the spirit, and I will sing with the understanding also.

Let's read those same two verses from *The Amplified Bible*:

1 CORINTHIANS 14:14,15 *(Amplified)*
14 For if I pray in an [unknown] tongue, my spirit [by

> the Holy Spirit within me] prays, but my mind is
> unproductive — bears no fruit and helps nobody.
> 15 Then what am I to do? I will pray with my spirit —
> by the Holy Spirit that is within me; but I will also pray
> intelligently — with my mind and understanding; I will
> sing with my spirit — by the Holy Spirit that is within
> me; but I will sing (intelligently) with my mind and
> understanding also.

Paul said, "I will pray with my spirit, and I will pray with my understanding." If praying in tongues is not for us today, then we would be extremely limited in praying in the Spirit.

And yet, we are spirit beings. We need to pray out of our spirits and not just out of our heads.

Paul is talking in these verses about two kinds of praying; mental praying and spiritual praying.

Mental praying with the understanding is praying out of our minds. While this is good and effective in many situations, it seems the church world as a whole has tried for too long to get by on mental praying alone.

Yet we cannot succeed with just mental praying alone. Why not? God's Word gives the answer in Romans 8:26.

ROMANS 8:26
26 Likewise the Spirit also helpeth our infirmities: for we know not what we should pray for as we ought: but the Spirit itself [Himself] maketh intercession for us with groanings which cannot be uttered.

There are times when we do not know for what to pray. It would be impossible in these situations for mental praying alone to get the job done. Spiritual praying is required.

Spiritual praying is praying out of your spirit in Spirit-given utterances. They can be utterances in your *known* language, or in a tongue that is *unknown* to you, or sometimes in *groanings.*

We may not always understand the entire situation surrounding a matter about which we are praying. But the Holy Spirit does. When we allow Him to pray through us, to help us in our prayer life, we will see amazing answers to our prayers.

Every Spirit-filled believer can expect the Holy Spirit to help him pray in the Spirit.

As I close this chapter I want to zero in on one of the two ways we can pray in the Spirit, and that is by praying in other tongues. I would like to share some specific benefits and uses of praying in the Spirit in other tongues.

Praying in Tongues To Magnify God

ACTS 10:46
46 For they heard them speak with tongues, and magnify God. . . .

Praying in tongues is a way in which we can magnify God.

For years as a minister, I had prayed — and had wonderful times in prayer. I used to go down to the barn and get up in the hay loft to pray — and I had marvelous times of prayer there.

But I went away from those times disappointed, although I was blessed. I would try to tell God how much I loved Him. I would use all the descriptive adjectives at my disposal to tell God how wonderful He is. I would

exhaust my vocabulary and leave that place of prayer
with my spirit feeling I had not said what I wanted to
say. My spirit felt cheated.

Now one of the things I appreciate most about being
filled with the Holy Spirit is praying with tongues. From
that day in 1937 when I was first Spirit-filled to this day,
I have worshiped and communicated with God, praying
and singing in tongues, every single day. And I never
have left that place of prayer feeling I didn't say what I
wanted to say, because my spirit was enabled by the Holy
Spirit who indwells me to say what it wanted to say.

If you are not doing so already, I invite you to come on
in and communicate with God supernaturally. God
wants to do so much more for you. He wants to communicate with you in a better way. Know the joy of fellowshiping with the Lord in the Spirit.

Praying in Tongues To Edify Yourself

JUDE 20
**20 But ye, beloved, building up yourselves on your
most holy faith, praying in the Holy Ghost.**

1 CORINTHIANS 14:4
**4   He that speaketh in an unknown tongue edifieth
himself. . . .**

There is one phase of speaking with tongues in our
prayer life that is not praying for someone else; it is not
interceding for anyone else. It is purely a means of per-
sonal spiritual edification. It aids us spiritually. It edifies
us. It builds us up. We all need this kind of praying. We
cannot help others; we cannot edify others unless we

ourselves have been edified.

Take time to build yourself up by praying much in the Holy Spirit — with other tongues.

Spiritual things are similar to natural things. Jesus used natural things to explain spiritual things.

In the natural, no one will be expert and keen in any area without working at it. In baseball, for instance, the good hitter did not get into his position without batting practice.

Likewise, things of the spirit don't fall on us like ripe cherries off a tree. We will not be expert in spiritual things unless we take time.

Praying in tongues will help you to be keen to spiritual things.

Praying in Tongues To Rest

ISAIAH 28:11,12

11 For with stammering lips and another tongue will he speak to this people.

12 To whom he said, This is the rest wherewith ye may cause the weary to rest; and this is the refreshing. . . .

Praying in tongues is a rest.

Howard Carter, who was one of the Pentecostal world's most renown teachers on the subject of spiritual gifts, said that speaking in tongues is a continual experience to assist us in the worship of God. It is a flowing stream that should never dry up. It will enrich your life spiritually. And it will enable you to help others and to work with God Himself in the consummation of His work in the earth through prayer.

Chapter 15

Quiet Prayer

One year my two children, Ken and Pat, studied by correspondence and my family traveled with me. We had a 43 feet long by 8 feet wide mobile home which we pulled with a pickup truck.

We were in California for a series of meetings when I was awakened suddenly in the night. I got up and checked the trailer doors thinking someone had come into the house. They were locked.

I checked Pat. She was sleeping soundly. I checked Ken. He was asleep. I came back to our bedroom and my wife was sleeping soundly.

So I lay down and began to pray in other tongues. I wasn't loud about it, but I did give expression to it.

The Bible speaks about not disturbing others in a church service. *"If any man speak in an unknown tongue, let it be by two, or at the most by three, and that by course; and let one interpret. But if there be no interpreter, let him keep silence in the church; and let him speak to himself, and to God"* (1 Cor. 14:27,28).

In other words, let him not speak out loud, but speak to himself and to God. You can sit there and talk to yourself and God without disturbing anyone. You can either whisper quietly, or you can pray on the inside of you.

That night, I did make audible sounds, but it was more of a whisper.

I began to look on the inside of me. And I picked up from my own spirit — my spirit is indwelled by the Holy

Spirit and it knows things — that something was wrong with someone in my family.

I said, "Who is it, Lord? What's wrong?"

Then by an inward intuition, not a voice, but by the inward intuition that every Christian ought to have, I knew a family member's life was in danger. You see, the Bible says as many as are led by the Spirit of God, they are the sons of God. And God's Spirit bears witness with our *spirit*; therefore, we are to be led by the Holy Spirit's witness in our spirit, which causes us to know things supernaturally.

I said, "Lord, I don't know who it is. I don't know for what to pray as I ought. But I'm going to trust the Holy Spirit to help me to make intercession." I lay there and prayed for nearly an hour in other tongues.

Then I had a note of victory. I knew that whatever I was praying for or about was settled. Very quietly, I sang in tongues, and laughed, then fell back to sleep.

Now this doesn't happen very often, but just before I woke up the next morning, I had a dream.

(God does speak to you in dreams sometimes. But let me say this lest folks get confused. Every time I've ever had a dream in which God spoke to me, the minute I awoke, I knew exactly what He was saying to me. If you think God spoke to you in a dream and you've got to run all over the country to find somebody to interpret it, forget it. It wasn't God. God is an intelligent Being. You are an intelligent being. If He can't get over to you what He's trying to say to you, forget it. Some people think every little dream they have is God trying to say something to them. And they're in confusion all the time, trying to figure out something.)

In this dream I knew I was in Shreveport, Louisiana. I was standing outside a hotel; I saw the sign giving the name of the hotel.

Suddenly, I was inside the hotel. My younger brother, Pat, was there. (Now although he had been saved and even filled with the Spirit, he was backslidden and wasn't living for God.) I saw that he took sick after midnight, in the early hours of morning.

He called the desk to tell them he was sick. Then he passed out. I saw an ambulance with red lights flashing come to take him to the hospital.

The scene changed. I was standing up against the wall in the corridor of a hospital. Across the hall there was a door. It was closed, but I knew my brother was behind it, and I knew a doctor was with him.

The doctor came out and shut the door behind him. He did not look up at me, but walked up in front of me and said, "He's dead."

In the dream, I said, "No, he's not."

Then the doctor looked up at me and said, "Well, I know better. I've pronounced too many people dead. He's dead."

I said, "No, he's not."

He said, "How do you know?"

I said, "The Lord Jesus told me."

"Oh," he said, "you're one of those nuts. I'll just show you."

He whirled around and opened the door. I followed him inside. A body lay on the table with a sheet pulled over it.

The doctor jerked the sheet down and said, "Just look!"

We looked. And my brother blinked his eyes! The doctor looked closer. My brother was breathing.

The doctor looked at me and said, "You must have known something I didn't know."

I said, "I surely did."

I woke up knowing that was what I had interceded for.

That happened in May. We went on preaching in California and finished in August. At the end of August we returned to our home in Texas, after having been gone 15 months.

We hadn't been back home 15 minutes — in fact, Ken and I were still parking the trailer in the back yard — when my brother, Pat, pulled into the drive.

He said to me, "I almost died while you were gone."

I said, "Yes, I know. It was last May, wasn't it?"

"Yes."

I said, "You were in Shreveport in a hotel. You took sick in the night. You called the operator, then passed out. They rushed you to the hospital. You were unconscious. The doctor told you afterwards that he thought for a while you were dead, didn't he?"

"Yes," he said. "Who told you? Momma?"

I said, "No. I haven't seen Momma. I haven't seen anyone. We just drove in here 20 minutes ago."

He said, "How did you know?"

I told him my experience.

He said, "That's exactly what happened."

Thank God for praying in tongues! This kind of praying belongs to us. This kind of praying is important. It is important to our own spiritual and physical lives. It is important in intercession for others and for the work of God in the earth. And it doesn't just belong to preachers.

Sometimes people feel that because they have to be so quiet about praying in certain places that it is not as expressive, or not as good, or not as powerful, or not as productive as otherwise. But it is.

I pray in tongues on airplanes. I pray very quietly, but it edifies me. It does something for my spirit. Now, I'm not usually interceding for anyone, but just worshiping God and building myself up spiritually. Even though I do it quietly, it is effective.

Likewise, my intercessory prayer for my brother was just as effective as I lay there on the bed beside my wife, that night in California, praying so quietly it did not disturb her.

Another time, we were preaching in Oregon. In the nighttime I was awakened. I thought I heard a door slam. Just my wife and I were in a smaller travel trailer this time. I got up and checked the doors; they were locked.

I lay back down and began to check inside my spirit. I knew prayer was needed, but I had no kind of intuition as to who or what it was.

I said, "Lord, I don't know what it is. But whatever it is, or whoever it is, somebody needs help. You said in Romans 8:26 that the Spirit helps us. So help me to make intercession."

I laid there and prayed very quietly for almost two hours. My wife slept right on by my side. Then I began to laugh and sing in tongues. I had a note of victory. I knew that whatever it was, I had the victory. I fell off to sleep.

I had no dream this time. I had no idea what it was.

Three days later someone came from the trailer park office saying we had an emergency long distance telephone call.

It was my sister, Oleta, calling from Texas. At first she was crying so I couldn't understand what she was saying. Finally I got her quieted down so I could tell what it was.

She said that Dub, our older brother, had broken his back. A woman had called her from a hospital in Kansas. The woman's husband was in the same room with Dub and he was going home. She was concerned that no one was there to see after Dub. He'd had an accident. He was in a cast because of the broken back and he was in a very low state physically. The doctors said they did not know if he was going to make it or not.

Oleta said, "I'm going to try to go up there, but I can't stay. What are we going to do? Can you come?"

I realized that was what I'd been praying about. And I knew I had the answer. How did I know? I just knew. I didn't have any gift of the Spirit in manifestation. By an inward witness I just knew.

I said, "Oleta, just forget it. Don't even go up there to see about him. He's going to make it. His back will be all right. I've already got the answer. In fact, he'll be home in a few days."

And that's what happened. With the doctors telling him he couldn't do it, Dub got up three days later and went to Texas. He was in our home when we got back.

I didn't even know for whom I was praying that

night — but the Spirit of God knew.

I did know that I was to pray.

Now I wake up every night and spend time talking in tongues. But I'm not praying about anybody else. I'm just fellowshiping with the Lord. I'm just communing with the Lord. I'm just worshiping the Lord. I'm just edifying my spirit. I'm just building myself up. But when I am awakened to make intercession, whether or not I know what it is about, I know it.

Usually, I lie there quietly and pray as I have shown you.

Some have asked, "Can you pray in tongues through your mind and never say anything?"

Actually, that's not praying in tongues — that's thinking in tongues.

You have to *say* it to pray. You may say it within yourself, but it isn't saying it in your mind, it is saying it in your *spirit*.

You may say it very quietly, but you are still saying it. And it is effective.

Chapter 16
Not-So-Quiet Prayer

There are times in prayer that you are almost forced into saying it out loud. Such pressure builds up within, it seems like if you don't say it, you will burst.

My wife and I married in November 1938. I pastored a little Full Gospel church. They had no parsonage. I'd been renting a room and boarding with one of the members.

My father-in-law, a farmer in the community, said, "When you get married, move in here. We've got plenty of room and you won't have to pay room and board. This will help you get started in life."

Four days after we were married, I moved my belongings into their big farmhouse.

About 9:30 that night, my father-in-law said, "Let's have family prayer."

They were Methodists. They were attending the Full Gospel church when I came to pastor it, but they were not "Pentecostal."

We all prayed out loud in English. They weren't very loud. And I was trying to be quiet.

I kept having an "urge" to pray in tongues and I didn't know whether or not they would like that. But it just kept building, and building, and building inside me, until finally I just threw caution to the wind, lifted my voice and prayed aloud in other tongues as hard and fast as I could.

I kept my eyes tightly shut because I didn't want to

see them. I just went after it. I groaned and prayed in tongues.

I know I could have kept from it to begin with, but once you yield to the Spirit, you get over into a supernatural flow and it's hard to stop.

After about 45 minutes of praying that way, the Lord spoke to me. Only I didn't know it was the Lord.

You see, I'd been filled with the Holy Spirit less than two years. And all they taught us in Pentecostal circles in those days was, get saved and baptized with the Holy Ghost. Then they turned you loose. We just had to stumble upon anything beyond that.

But I realize now that it was the Lord who spoke these words to me, "Lay your hand on your wife and I'll fill her with the Holy Ghost."

I thought, *Well, what if I were to lay my hand on her and nothing happened?*

So I just kept praying, thinking that would go away.

Again it came, "Lay your hand on your wife and I'll fill her with the Holy Ghost."

I ignored it and went on praying.

The third time, "Lay your hand on your wife and I'll fill her with the Holy Ghost."

I opened my eyes and looked at my father-in-law kneeling to my right, and then to my wife, kneeling to my left, and then to my mother-in-law, on the other side of my wife.

I know what I said is unbelief, but God will put up with a little unbelief in you when you don't know any better. But you can't get by with that later on. This was new to me.

I said, "It won't hurt to try it."

Then I reached my left hand out and laid it on top of her head.

She had no instructions. She never sought the baptism in the Holy Spirit a day in her life. I didn't tell her to do anything. I just laid my hand on top of her head and the minute I touched her, she lifted both hands automatically and started talking fluently in tongues.

I looked at my watch to see what time it was. She talked in tongues an hour and a half and sang three songs in other tongues. We had Pentecost in that Methodist home!

About midnight the Spirit of God spoke to me in the same voice and told me how to deal with my mother-in-law and she'd be healed. She had a double goiter. She had her suitcase packed to enter the hospital the next morning to undergo surgery.

She had no faith for healing. That is obvious. She wouldn't have had her suitcase packed to go to the hospital if she expected to be healed.

But the Spirit of the Lord told me what to do and that she'd be healed.

I did. He did. And she was. She never had the operation.

I realized afterwards what actually happened that night. What I was doing in the Spirit was praying for my wife and for my mother-in-law.

The Spirit of God led me to pray for them. I prayed as hard and fast as I could in other tongues and with groanings for 45 to 50 minutes. I concluded by singing in tongues and laughing in the Spirit. About that time is when the Lord by the Spirit said, "Lay your hand on your wife and I'll fill her." Then He told me how to deal with my mother-in-law, and that part of the goiter on the outside went down like you'd stuck a pin in a balloon.

Chapter 17
Groanings in the Spirit

One way the Holy Spirit helps us in prayer is in groaning — and also in praying in other tongues.

People often quote Romans 8:26 and 27 in reference to the Holy Spirit's part in intercession. Yet to quote these two verses alone does not give their full meaning. They are linked to the verses before them.

I will print the entire passage here with capital letters to show continuity:

ROMANS 8:22-27
22 For we know that the whole creation GROANETH AND TRAVAILETH IN PAIN [Hold that in your mind; all these verses speak of groanings.] **together until now.**
23 And not only they, BUT OURSELVES ALSO, which have the firstfruits of the Spirit, EVEN WE OUR-SELVES GROAN WITHIN OURSELVES, waiting for the adoption, to wit, the redemption of our body.
24 For we are saved by hope: but hope that is seen is not hope: for what a man seeth, why doth he yet hope for? [This is not speaking about the new birth. It is written to people already born again. It is talking about hoping for the fullness of redemption when we have a new body.]
25 But if we hope for that we see not, then do we with patience wait for it.
26 LIKEWISE [or in the same manner, the Spirit helps us by groanings] **THE SPIRIT ALSO HELPETH OUR INFIR-MITIES: for we know not what we should pray for as we ought: but the Spirit itself** [Himself] **MAKETH INTERCESSION FOR US WITH GROANINGS WHICH CANNOT BE UTTERED.**
27 And he that searcheth the hearts knoweth what is

**the mind of the Spirit, BECAUSE HE MAKETH INTER-
CESSION FOR THE SAINTS ACCORDING TO THE
WILL OF GOD.**

All the creation is groaning and travailing in pain. The
ultimate consciousness of pain resides in God because of His
perfect love. Through our fellowship with God we are brought
into fellowship with the suffering creation. Our consciousness
of the groaning of the creation is much more acute than when
we were outside the Kingdom of God, because we are united to
God through Jesus Christ (John 15:5).

The Holy Spirit interprets to us God's consciousness of suffering and makes intercession with groanings that cannot be
uttered.

— Reidt

The late P. C. Nelson was a noted linguist. Some 30
years ago, a secular magazine called him the leading
authority of the day on Greek and the second-ranked
authority on Hebrew. He could read and write 32 lan-
guages.

Nelson said that the Greek in Romans 8:26 actually
implies, "with groanings that cannot be uttered in articulate speech."

They are uttered — but not in articulate speech.
Articulate speech is your regular speech. These groanings — I know both from the Bible and from experience — come from within you, out of your spirit, but to
be effective they must escape your lips.

Again it is the Holy Spirit helping you to pray. You
just cannot express them in your own words.

The New English Bible translates it, ". . . through our
inarticulate groans the Spirit himself is pleading for us."

The *Phillips* translation calls them ". . . agonizing
longings which never find words."

We may not know how or what to ask in prayer so that our prayer will correspond with our real needs. The Holy Spirit moves us with groanings which we cannot express in words and helps us direct our desires to the proper objects. Also to help us to be specific is a part of the groanings. These groanings, yearnings, are according to the will of God and express His care for us. Although we cannot understand the groanings (Greek, sigh), they are intelligible to God. He always responds. In adverse circumstances or conditions the Holy Spirit intercedes with groanings.

— Reidt

I've noticed in my own life that sometimes I go along and don't have too much of this. There is no particular need for it at the moment. But then, in time of adverse circumstances or conditions, those groanings begin to well up inside me — that is the Holy Spirit helping us to pray.

You yield yourself to the Spirit in prayer and He uses you in this manner.

Take note of the word "likewise" in Romans 8:26. It means "in the same manner."

In the same manner as what? In the same manner as what was said before.

In other words, just as the whole creation groaneth and travaileth in pain, even we ourselves groan within ourselves. *"LIKEWISE the Spirit also helpeth our infirmities . . .* [and] *maketh intercession for us with groanings which cannot be uttered"* (Rom. 8:26).

Until everything does come into complete harmony with the will of God, as Wilford Reidt said:

There will always be the need for the Holy Spirit to intercede with groanings. We may know the will of God but only the Holy Spirit knows how to effectively present the need. There are circumstances in which we are not sure of how to pray. We need the groaning of the Holy Spirit in intercession.

— Reidt

Chapter 18
The Praying Church

And whether one member suffer, all the members suffer with it. . . .

— 1 Corinthians 12:26

Effective prayer will bring deliverance. We are members one of another. As the Body of Christ and as members, we should partake in the healing of each other. We weep with those who weep — then we rejoice with those who rejoice (Rom. 12:15).

ROMANS 15:1
1 We then that are strong ought to bear the infirmities of the weak, and not to please ourselves.

How do we bear the infirmities of the weak? To answer that question we must also ask for the meaning of "bear" and of "infirmities."

"Bear" means to lift with the idea of removing.

"Infirmities" means in this setting "a scruple of conscience." Therefore it is not a physical thing, but something wrong in their belief.

— Reidt

In the surrounding scriptures, Paul discussed the fact that some people felt it was wrong to eat meat, because sometimes the blood of animals sold in the marketplace for meat had been offered to idols.

Paul said that there was only one God, and these meats were not offered to our Father God. But yet, if eating meat offered to idols would cause his brother to offend, he wouldn't eat it as long as the world stands. Then he gives Romans 15:1.

A scruple of conscience is involved. They are brothers, but they are weak. Our prayers on their behalf can help bring them to a realization of the truth.

The Ephesian Prayers

Ephesians 1:17-23 and 3:14-21 are Holy Spirit-given prayers which apply to the Church everywhere.

The turning point in my life came when I prayed them a thousand times or more for myself. I would kneel, open my Bible, and say, "Father, I am praying these prayers for myself. Because they are Spirit-given prayers, this has to be Your will for me just as it was Your will for the Church at Ephesus. . . ."

Then I would continue just as the prayers read except where Paul said, "you," I would substitute "me," like this:

> God, of our Lord Jesus Christ, the Father of glory,
>
> Give unto me the spirit of wisdom and revelation in the knowledge of Him,
>
> The eyes of my understanding being enlightened;
>
> That I may know what is the hope of His calling, and what is the riches of the glory of His inheritance in the saints,
>
> And what is the exceeding greatness of His power to usward who believe, according to the working of His mighty power,
>
> Which He wrought in Christ, when He raised Him from the dead, and set Him at His own right hand in the heavenly places. . . .

After about six months, the first thing I was praying for started happening. The revelation of God's Word began to come.

Now that is how those prayers worked when I prayed them for myself. The subject of this book is prayer — both for oneself and for others. Therefore, I also have prayed these same prayers for Christians who do not see certain Bible truths.

I pray these prayers for them every morning and night. I use their name, like this:

> Lord, I am praying this prayer for Joe. God of our Lord Jesus Christ, the Father of glory, give unto Joe the spirit of wisdom and revelation in the knowledge of Him:
>
> I pray that the eyes of Joe's understanding be enlightened; that Joe may know what is the hope of His calling, and what is the riches of the glory of His inheritance in the saints. . . .

I prayed ten days for one relative, morning and night. With no human teacher talking to him (he was a Spirit-filled Christian), he wrote me, "It's amazing how things have opened up to me. I'm beginning to see what you've been talking about."

You see, God has already blessed us with all spiritual blessings in heavenly places in Christ Jesus (Eph. 1:3). Some Christians just don't know it, so they can't take advantage of it. They suffer from the infirmity of not knowing.

We can pray these prayers in Ephesians for them. It is necessary to stay with it — morning and night, and more often if possible.

Bearing One Another's Burdens

GALATIANS 6:2
**2   Bear ye one another's burdens, and so fulfil the law
of Christ.**

Prayer is involved in bearing one another's burdens.
Remember that "bear" means to lift with the idea of
removing. Prayer is one way we can lift with the idea of
removing burdens people are carrying.

HEBREWS 12:1,2
**1   Wherefore seeing we also are compassed about with
so great a cloud of witnesses, let us lay aside every
weight, and the sin which doth so easily beset us, and
let us run with patience the race that is set before us,
2   Looking unto Jesus, the author and finisher of our
faith; who for the joy that was set before him endured
the cross, despising the shame, and is set down at the
right hand of the throne of God.**

This talks about two things which hinder Christians
in the race we are running — weights and sins. (What
may be a weight to one, may not be a weight to another.)
We can help fellow believers to run their races better
by helping to lift these burdens through prayer. We don't
need to criticize them; we need to pray for them.
When we take our places in prayer for each other, we
are helping the entire body to come into maturity.

Chapter 19
Until Christ Be Formed in You

My little children, of whom I travail in birth again until Christ be formed in you.
— Galatians 4:19

Paul had travailed — groaned and prayed in other tongues — for these people, and they were born again. (Travail carries the idea of a woman travailing in birth with pain and agony and groanings.)

Now Paul says he is travailing *again* until Christ be formed in you.

He travailed for them as sinners to be birthed into the Kingdom of God — now he is travailing for them as Christians that they might become mature, that they might grow up and not be baby Christians.

There is a similarity between spiritual growth and physical growth. No one is born a full-grown human. In the natural, people are born babies and they grow up. No one is born a full-grown Christian. They are born babies. Then they are to grow up, spiritually.

The Bible says, *"As newborn babes, desire the sincere milk of the word, that ye may grow thereby"* (1 Peter 2:2).

These churches of Galatia were trying to get back under the law instead of walking on in grace. Paul was alarmed. So he was praying and travailing for them that they mature and grow.

Epaphras did the same thing for the Colossian Christians and those in Laodicea and Hierapolis.

COLOSSIANS 4:12,13
12 Epaphras, who is one of you, a servant of Christ,
saluteth you, always labouring fervently for you in
prayers, that ye may stand perfect [mature] and complete in all the will of God.
13 For I bear him record, that he hath a great zeal for
you, and them that are in Laodicea, and them in Hierapolis.

The *Centenary Translation of the New Testament*
translates verse 12 like this: "Epaphras, one of yourselves, salutes you, a slave of Christ who is always agonizing for you in his prayers, that you may stand firm,
mature, and fully assured in all the will of God."

I remember particularly the wonderful experience
with God a young woman had when she came to the
altar during a revival meeting I was holding. She was
gloriously saved and gloriously baptized in the Holy
Spirit. Oh! What a glow was upon her face.

Just a little less than a year later, I was back in the
area and I inquired about her because of the very
unusual and marvelous experience she'd had with God.

"Oh," they said, with their faces dark and frowning,
"she's backslidden."

I said, "Oh, I hate that."

They said, "Yes, we do, too."

Then, just as plainly, the Spirit of God spoke up on
the inside of me and said, "Yes, and the church is to
blame for it. The church is responsible for it."

I couldn't understand that for the longest time. How
could the church be responsible for somebody's backslid-
ing?

Then I saw it in Galatians 4:19: *"My little children, of*

whom I travail in birth again until Christ be formed in you."

You see, that church just saw her get saved and baptized in the Holy Spirit. Then they said, "Well, she's got it made now."

But she was a baby. They should have continued to hold her up in prayer. Because they did not, when Judgment Day comes, God will hold that church responsible. He is going to require of every church responsibility for the babies born at its altars.

"What did you do with them?" will be the question. "Did you teach them? Did you continue to pray for them? Or, if they made a mistake, did you knock them down and say, 'You backslidden buzzard, get right with God or get out of here — one of the two'?"

While people are babies spiritually, somebody has to carry them. Somebody has to feed them. Somebody has to care for them.

This is one place where prayer comes in.

Older believers need to hold them up in prayer as they're learning to walk.

When my children or grandchildren fell as they were learning to walk, I didn't slap them. I got hold of them and loved them and said, "Just keep at it, honey. You'll learn."

In many cases, in praying for Christians, such travail is not necessary, because they are not so tightly bound as the Galatian church seemed to be.

Learn to listen to the Spirit of God and pray as He directs.

Chapter 20
Praying for Those in Sin

*And lest, when I come again, my God will hum-
ble me among you, and that I shall bewail many
which have sinned already, and have not repented
of the uncleanness and fornication and lasciviousness which they have committed.*

— 2 Corinthians 12:21

We have already seen that we are to travail in birth
again when necessary in order for Christ to be formed in
believers.

Paul here said that he would "bewail" many who have
sinned and have not repented. We need to make intercession for those who have sinned and not repented.

Corinth was one of the most licentious and immoral
cities in that part of the world. The same spirits that
prevailed in the city got into the church. When Paul
named uncleanness, fornication, and lasciviousness, he
was talking about sexual impurities. People in the
church had done these things and had not repented.

The Greek word translated "bewail" means to
grieve — it is the feeling or the act of grieving. Here to
bewail includes both the feeling and the act of grieving.
The act of grieving is a response in intercessory prayer.

Worrell's translation sheds light on Paul's meaning.

2 CORINTHIANS 12:21 *(Worrell)*
**21 Lest, when I come again, my God should humble me
before you, and I should mourn for many of those who**

**have heretofore sinned, and repented not of the
uncleanness, and fornication and lasciviousness which
they practiced.**

We live in a world and an age of permissiveness and
immorality. Many things such as homosexuality, living
together without marriage, and all uncleanness along
these lines have come out of hiding.

The Church seems to have winked at some of these
things. But we are to feel toward sin just like God does.

> Sin is a violation of the will of God. God is perpetually at
> war with sin. We use sin in its broad form that includes iniq-
> uity and transgression (1 John 3:4; 5:17). Sin leads to death
> (James 1:13-15). Death is separation from God. We are not
> talking of physical death.
>
> Sin is a hideous thing. Some men of God have expressed
> their feelings about it in strong language. Chrysostom (347-
> 407 A.D.) said, "I preach and think it is more bitter to sin
> against Christ than to suffer the torments of hell." Anselm
> (11th century) said, "If hell were on one side, and sin on the
> other, I would rather leap into hell than willingly sin against
> my God."
>
> Where are the heroes, "Who resist unto blood, striving
> against sin?" (Heb. 12:4).
>
> . . . We only know God's estimate of sin by the magnitude
> of the sacrifice He has provided to atone for it, His Son!
>
> — Reidt

2 CORINTHIANS 5:10,11
**10 For we must all appear before the judgment seat of
Christ; that every one may receive the things done in
his body, according to that he hath done, whether it be
good or bad.**
**11 Knowing therefore the terror of the Lord, we per-
suade men. . . .**

God is love. I preach faith — and faith works by love — so I have to preach love. But if we are not careful, we preach in such a manner that people forget God is also a God of judgment. He is also a God of justice. Sin has a penalty.

Paul grieved over the Corinthian Christians who had sinned and had not repented. No wonder. We should be grieved for those among us who are in the same situation.

Wilford Reidt said, "The awfulness of sin and its consequences should cause us to intercede for men."

Then, too, in the category of sin, God supplied a list in Revelation 21:8. He listed fear and unbelief at the top of the list — even before murder.

Seeing our brethren caught up in these snares of fear, unbelief, doubt, unforgiveness, worry, and so forth should compel us to intercede for them.

Chapter 21
Praying for Deliverance

Finally, brethren, pray for us, that the word of the Lord may have free course, and be glorified, even as it is with you: AND THAT WE MAY BE DELIVERED from unreasonable and wicked men: for all men have not faith. But the Lord is faithful, who shall stablish you, and keep you from evil.
— 2 Thessalonians 3:1-3

This verse says, ". . . *PRAY for us . . . that we may be delivered. . . .*"

In order to carry out Paul's prayer request, the Thessalonians would have had to pray for Paul's deliverance and protection.

Many are the accounts I know of firsthand — some from our own experience and others from people we know — where because of prayer, people were delivered.

Wilford Reidt knew personally a mother God awakened at 2 o'clock in the morning to pray for her son. She knew from the urgency of the Spirit that something was seriously wrong. She did not quench that urgency, but yielded to it. She earnestly gave herself to prayer until the burden lifted. Later she learned that at the moment God called her to pray, the ship her son was on was struck by lightning. The medics on the warship laid her son out for dead — and put his body with others in a place for the dead. He surprised them some time later by reviving. He is alive today because his mother prayed.

I heard Brother T., an old-time Pentecostal minister and missionary, tell something that happened when he and his wife, Blanche, were in Africa as missionaries.

His wife's parents lived on a farm in the New England states. Her father, Brother G., had been an unsaved alcoholic, dying with cirrhosis of the liver, when he was carried into one of Sister Woodworth-Etter's meetings and marvelously healed, saved, and filled with the Holy Spirit.

At the time of this happening, Brother G.'s daughter, Blanche, and son-in-law were in Africa as missionaries. Before sunup one morning Brother G. headed for the barn to milk the cows. Halfway between the barn and the house at about 5 o'clock, he set down the milk pails and came back into the kitchen.

His wife looked up from cooking breakfast. "What's wrong? You look pale. Are you sick?"

He said, "No, I'm not sick."

She said, "What's the matter?"

He said, "I don't know what it is, but something's wrong with Blanche. Her life is in danger. Let's pray."

He fell down on the kitchen floor and began to groan in the spirit and pray with tongues.

Six o'clock came. He still was praying.

Seven o'clock came. He still was praying.

Eight o'clock. The cows were lowing. The chicks were cackling; the pigs were squealing; they hadn't been fed. Still he prayed, groaning and agonizing.

Nine o'clock. Ten o'clock. Eleven o'clock. Blanche's father, old Brother G., 82 years old, still hadn't gotten up from the floor.

Twelve o'clock. One o'clock. He still prayed.

Two o'clock in the afternoon. Nine hours without stopping, groaning, crying, and praying. Then at two o'clock the burden lifted. He laughed and sang in tongues.

"Whatever it is," he said to his wife praying with him, "we've got it!"

Communications were not what they are today. In the process of time, a letter came by boat from Africa.

I heard Brother T. tell what he'd written in that letter to his wife's parents.

"I wrote to tell them that Blanche contracted a tropical fever," he said.

It was the kind of fever that when you got it, you did not survive.

He told how Blanche had indeed gone right down to the place of death. In fact, she was left for dead. But suddenly, she rose up well!

Eventually, Blanche's parents and Brother T. compared notes. Allowing for the difference in time, the exact time Blanche rose up well was at 2 o'clock, when the burden left her father.

Blanche's father, Brother G., had wrestled with this prayer burden for nine hours. That's persistence. He had refused to give up until the burden lifted.

Now — here is something many have missed. *God help us to see it.*

Let me say it again, we emphasize faith and the prayer of faith endeavoring to get people to believe God "now" for their own individual healing. But we do not mean to leave the impression that that is the only kind of praying.

In crusades and seminars, for example, we endeavor to get people to the position of faith right now to receive their own immediate needs. We are dealing with people who are there for their own individual needs to be met.

The laws that govern the operation of the prayer of faith do not govern the operation of the prayer of intercession.

The prayer of faith is prayed primarily for yourself.

It is not often you can pray the prayer of faith for someone else — unless they are bona fide baby Christians. You can carry them temporarily on your faith, in some instances.

If Brother G. had not known something about prevailing prayer — the prayer that persists until victory is gained — if he had simply heard about the prayer of faith, which is right and legitimate, he might have said to his wife, "We don't know what it is. But whatever it is, let's just agree that Blanche will be all right."

That would not have worked. Their daughter, Blanche, would have died.

The prayer of faith doesn't always work in every situation. It isn't designed to — if it were, that would be the only prayer we'd ever need to pray. We wouldn't need all the other kinds of praying that the Spirit of God through the Word encourages people to pray.

I can always pray the prayer of faith for myself. And I do that. But I cannot always pray the prayer of faith for the other fellow.

Sometimes I can — if I can get him to agree with me. If he is not present, how can I get him to agree with me?

Great victories have been won through prayer.

Great battles have been lost because we did not take

time to pray.

In 1965 I preached a six-week meeting in Oklahoma. Then I drove back to my home near Dallas to take care of some business before driving to Kansas City to speak at a Full Gospel Business Men's banquet.

When I got home I had a burden to pray for someone. I had the sensation of someone's being thrown from an automobile. But I had so much business to attend to in a short time that I got to thinking, *I've got to do this, and that, and the other,* and I let it slip by me.

I did pray silently. But I should have taken time to really get quiet and alone with God to find out, *Why is this coming to me? What is this?* I should have taken time to get over into the spirit realm out beyond the natural realm.

It was raining when we left Dallas on Friday. We had seat belts in the car, but I never wore them. This time, I fastened my seat belt.

My wife said, "What is it?" She knew I never did that.

I said, "I don't know. I had the sensation of someone being thrown out of the car, and I thought it might be us."

We prayed in a general way and claimed protection.

We spent the night in Tulsa with friends. When we left on Saturday morning, it still was raining.

Again, I fastened my seat belt because I couldn't get away from that sensation. I should have taken time to pray about it, but I did not.

We were in Kansas City on Saturday night, actually eating at the banquet just before I was to speak, when someone came with the message that I had a long distance phone call.

I went to the phone. Our son told me that my niece had had an accident and was thrown through the windshield. The doctors didn't give her a chance to live.

That's what God was trying to tell me.

We talk about the times we listened — but there are times we did not. Why hadn't I taken the time? I was too busy to assume the responsibility.

What an awesome responsibility. Lives oftentimes hinge on our praying.

What would have happened if I had taken the time to pray? She would have avoided that accident.

What did happen? She died at 25 leaving two children, ages 3 and 5.

In 1939 my wife and I had accepted another pastorate and had moved away, but we were back in the area where we'd first lived, visiting my wife's parents.

We went with them to visit a neighboring farmer. He'd been sickly, but they hadn't discovered exactly what was wrong. They knew it was serious.

The women were in the house. This farmer, my father-in-law, and I were sitting on the front porch, talking.

On the inside of me, I had a burden, an agony really, to pray for this farmer. As he and my father-in-law talked, the man opened the door by something he said so I could move right in and say something to him about the Lord. But I didn't. I held my peace. Then the conversation changed. And I never could work it around again. I said nothing to him about his spiritual welfare.

We spent another day or two with my wife's folks,

then came on home. A couple of days later, my mother-in-law called and said this man had died.

I regretted for a while that I hadn't followed up on the leading of the Lord and said something to him. Then I thought no more about it.

Sunday night, as was our custom, we met at the altar to pray 15 minutes before the service.

I stepped off the platform, knelt, and had just shut my eyes when I was in the Spirit. I saw that man. I shall never forget it. It took me weeks to get away from it. I'd wake up in the night and see it. I saw this man in hell. I saw the fires of hell boiling up around him. I heard his screams. I heard him cry out like the rich man did for water to cool his tongue.

Then I saw Jesus. He pointed at me and said, "I'm going to hold you responsible for him. I gave you a burden of prayer and you didn't pray. I opened the door for you to talk and you didn't talk."

"Oh, my God!" I cried. With tears, on my knees for an hour and a half, I repented, crying, "Oh, God. Let that thing pass from me."

I didn't preach that night. The others didn't know what was happening.

> We should never take an urge to pray lightly. It may make the difference between life and death to some other soldier of the cross.
>
> — Reidt

Chapter 22
Interceding for the Lost

Who hath heard such a thing? who hath seen such things? Shall the earth be made to bring forth in one day? or shall a nation be born at once? for as soon as Zion travailed, she brought forth her children.

— Isaiah 66:8

Many have looked at this verse and thought it referred only to the rebirth of Israel as a nation. Yet most Old Testament prophecy has a twofold application — first the natural, then the spiritual. Isaiah is prophesying that Israel will be reborn as a nation in the natural, and that in the spiritual, Zion will travail and bring forth her children.

Who is Zion?

The New Testament tells us that the New Covenant believer is not come to Mount Sinai where Moses received the Ten Commandments under the Old Covenant — but that we are come to Mount Zion. It calls the Church, Mount Zion.

HEBREWS 12:18-24
18 For ye are not come unto the mount that might be touched, and that burned with fire, nor unto blackness, and darkness, and tempest,
19 And the sound of a trumpet, and the voice of words; which voice they that heard intreated that the word should not be spoken to them any more:

20 (For they could not endure that which was commanded, And if so much as a beast touch the mountain,
it shall be stoned, or thrust through with a dart:
21 And so terrible was the sight, that Moses said, I
exceedingly fear and quake:)
22 BUT YE ARE COME UNTO MOUNT SION, and unto
the city of the living God, the heavenly Jerusalem, and
to an innumerable company of angels,
23 TO THE GENERAL ASSEMBLY AND CHURCH OF
THE FIRSTBORN, which are written in heaven, and to
God the Judge of all, and to the spirits of just men
made perfect,
24 And to Jesus the mediator of the new covenant, and
to the blood of sprinkling, that speaketh better things
than that of Abel.

Notice this calls the Church of the general assembly
of the firstborn, "Mount Zion." And our text in Isaiah
66:8 said that, ". . . *as soon as Zion travailed, she
brought forth her children.*"

GALATIANS 4:19
19 My little children, of whom I travail in birth again
until Christ be formed in you.

Paul is writing to the churches throughout Galatia
(Gal. 1:2). He intimates that he travailed in birth for
them to be saved in the beginning. (Now he is travailing
"again.")

We talk about making conversions. God does not mention conversions — He wants births. You *must be born
again!*

You cannot have births without having travail. The
picture here is of a woman having a baby.

(Now I do not mean that one must come to the altar

and travail to be born again. The baby does not birth itself. But for true births out of the kingdom of darkness and into the kingdom of light, some person, somewhere, has travailed.)

> Paul travailed. It was a spiritual activity. It is an intense suffering in the inner man. It is comparable to the pangs of natural childbirth. It involves real intercession. I had a friend, now with the Lord, who travailed in prayer and intercession until you would think his heart would break literally. Sure it is hard on the outer man.
>
> — Reidt

I've been there myself, again and again. I could give any number of illustrations. This is one of the most outstanding, however.

It happened the first Friday night of December 1953 in Phoenix, Arizona, where I was conducting a meeting.

During the meeting I stayed in the home of one of the families in the church. After the Friday night service they invited their three married daughters and their husbands to come to the home for refreshments and a time of visiting.

We men were seated in the living room talking. The women were in the kitchen preparing to serve the food.

Suddenly, I had an urge to pray. Now, don't misunderstand me; nobody made me do it, but there was a burden about it. An urge to pray just seemed to fall upon me.

I knew these folks would understand such a thing. (If they would not have, I would have excused myself and gone to the privacy of my bedroom to pray.) So I said to our host, "I've got to pray, and I have to pray now."

Brother F. called the ladies from the kitchen, "Just

forget about the food. Brother Hagin's got a burden to pray. Let's all just join him."

I knelt beside a large chair in the living room. The moment my knees touched the floor I was in the Spirit. I lifted my voice, praying in other tongues and groanings.

It seemed like down deep within me I was hurting so badly I was about to deliver a baby. In travail there's pain — there are groanings.

I knew I was interceding. When that spirit of intercession for the lost is upon you, you'll feel within your own being that you are lost. You know you are not. You know you are a child of God. But you take upon yourself the condition the other person is in. That person is lost. So you feel lost.

I've had people come to me many times saying something like this, "Brother Hagin, I know I'm saved and filled with the Holy Spirit, but sometimes in the service when God begins to move, I start to feel on the inside just like I'm lost myself. When the altar call is given, I wonder if I should go to the altar myself. I wonder if perhaps I'm not right with God."

"That's intercession," I explain to them. "That's the Spirit of God trying to roll the burden of some lost soul off on someone. He was searching through the congregation to find someone He could use.

"When that happens again, if you can't contain yourself, and the service is still going on, get up and go to a place of prayer. Otherwise, sit there quietly and groan within yourself, until the person you are interceding for responds to the call of God."

There is something out here in this area that we need

to learn again. The art of intercession is a lost art among us. We'll never really have the depth of the move of the Spirit of God until we have that kind of intercession.

I prayed that Friday night in Phoenix with groanings, and tears, and other tongues for about an hour. I knew I was interceding for someone who was lost. And I knew to keep at it until I had a note of victory.

(A note of victory — that is when the burden lifts, and you feel light, wonderful, and blessed. Or, when you begin to sing in other tongues. Or, when you begin to laugh instead of groan. In other words, you have whatever it is you are praying about.)

Once in a great while, the Lord will let me know what or whom I am praying about. That Friday night, He let me know. He gave me a vision.

I saw the church where I was holding a meeting full of people.

I saw myself at the pulpit preaching.

I heard myself preach a sermon I'd never preached before. I heard myself give four points to this sermon. (I got a brand new sermon which I preached the following Sunday night.)

I saw myself finish the sermon, then lean over the pulpit and point to a man sitting the second seat from the front.

I heard myself say as I pointed to him, "Friend, God shows me you are past 70 years and that you've been brought up to believe that there is no hell. But He told me to tell you that you have one foot in hell right now, and the other one is slipping in."

I saw that man leave the pew, come and kneel at the

altar, and be saved.

I knew I was making intercession for him. I knew I was travailing in prayer for him.

The folks present knew I'd seen something. So they asked me. I told them. I described the man to them. I described how he was dressed.

The following Sunday night everything came to pass exactly as I had seen it on the preceding Friday.

Those people who had prayed with me told me after the service, "Brother Hagin, we had that fellow located before you ever got to the service. He was sitting where you said he'd be sitting. He was dressed just the way you saw him. We'd never seen him before." Nobody in that church had ever seen him. So they wouldn't have known to pray. But the Holy Spirit knew.

The man was saved along with others. After the service he came to hug the pastor and me.

He said to the pastor, "This preacher here said I was past 70. I'm 72. This is the first time I've ever been inside a church building. The preacher said I was raised to believe there is no hell. My parents were Universalists. They taught me that there is no hell.

"This preacher told me that God told him to tell me I had one foot in hell and the other was slipping. I know exactly what He meant. That's one reason why I came to Phoenix. I'm from up north where it's cold. But I had a severe heart attack and my doctor thought it would help my health to come here."

Somebody said, "He got saved Sunday night." But it really happened on Friday night when I was travailing in birth.

Do you know why babies are not being born into churches today? (Oh, some have a lot of conversions, but few births.) It is because there is no travail — no groanings.

And when some people begin to travail and groan in prayer, others are ready to throw them out.

Years ago, I ministered in a Full Gospel church that was running several hundred in the Sunday morning services. And on Sunday night the building was almost full.

They had a dear old lady, dear old Grandma Greer, who was at that time 80 some odd years of age. She'd been in Pentecost since the turn of the century. Way back around 1906 she had been baptized in the Holy Spirit. She knew something about travailing and waiting on God. (The old-timers did.) She would pray at the altar, groaning and praying in other tongues in the spirit of travail — carrying the entire thing, probably, on her own back.

Three years later I came back to this same church. Instead of having the building full for Sunday morning services, they had about 80 or 90 people. On Sunday night they had 35 to 50.

"What happened?" I asked someone.

One of the members said, "Do you remember old Grandma Greer?"

"Yes."

"Well, she was at the altar praying like she always did, and the new pastor got up and said, 'We're not going to have any of that around here.'"

He put a stop to it. They had no more babies being born, because there was no travailing. When Zion travails she brings forth her children.

Chapter 23
Prevailing in Prayer

To effectively prevail in prayer, your prayer must be based on God's Word. Faith can only begin where the will of God is known, and God's Word *is* His will. In the ninth chapter of Daniel and the second verse, we see that Daniel realized from reading God's Word that the seventy-year captivity of Jerusalem which had been prophesied by Jeremiah was soon to be completed.

DANIEL 9:2
2 In the first year of his reign I Daniel understood by books the number of the years, whereof the word of the Lord came to Jeremiah the prophet, that he would accomplish seventy years in the desolations of Jerusalem.

As a result of what Daniel read in God's Word, he set his face to seek the Lord through fasting and prayer. It was three full weeks, however, before an angel came with the answer Daniel was seeking.

Daniel's prayer was heard the first day he prayed. The angel told him:

DANIEL 10:12
12 ... from the first day that thou didst set thine heart to understand, and to chasten thyself before thy God, thy words were heard, and I am come for thy words.

In the next verse, the angel disclosed the secret of why it took so long for Daniel's prayer to be answered:

"But THE PRINCE OF THE KINGDOM OF PERSIA WITHSTOOD ME one and twenty days: but, lo, Michael, one of the chief princes, came to help me . . ." (v. 13).

Let's look back at the first verse of this chapter: *"In the third year of Cyrus king of Persia a thing was revealed unto Daniel. . . ."* These events, then, are dated as having happened during the third year of the reign of Cyrus, *king* of Persia. Cyrus was a man who sat on the throne of the kingdom of Persia.

But in the 13th verse, the angel said, "the *prince* of Persia withstood me." This prince of Persia fought up in the heavenlies, against God's message-bearing angel. Reinforcements — Michael the archangel — had to come to help the angel get through with that message to Daniel! This prince of Persia was a spirit being.

We see from this passage of Scripture, among others, that *there is a double-kingdom system.*

There is a *seen* kingdom upon the earth with human rulers. But behind that earthly kingdom (or nation) is an *unseen* kingdom with a satanic ruler.

This explains something about the temptation of Jesus.

LUKE 4:5,6
5   And the devil, taking him [Jesus] up into an high mountain, shewed unto him all the kingdoms of the world in a moment of time.
6   And the devil said unto him, All this power will I give thee, and the glory of them: For THAT IS DELIVERED UNTO ME; and to whomsoever I will I give it.

What power is being discussed here? The power of the nations of this world!

Some have suggested the devil didn't have that power or authority. If so, wouldn't Jesus have known that and told him so?

The Bible says this was a temptation. If the devil *didn't* have that power and authority, it couldn't have been a temptation — and the Son of God would have been partner to a lie and a fraud. But it was a *bona fide* temptation.

Where, then, did Satan get that authority? Did God give it to him?

God made the world and the fullness thereof. Then He made His man Adam. And this is what a lot of people — including ministers — haven't seen. God said, "Adam, I give you dominion over all the works of my hands" (Ps. 8:6). In one sense, God was saying, "Adam, you're the god of this world. You run it." *God gave the world to Adam!*

But the New Testament calls Satan the god of this world (2 Cor. 4:4). When did Satan become the god of this world? When Adam sinned. It was when Adam committed high treason and sold out to Satan.

Notice what Satan said to Jesus: ". . . *All this power will I give thee, and the glory of them* [the kingdoms of the world]: *FOR THAT IS DELIVERED UNTO ME . . .*" (Luke 4:6). Who delivered it to Satan? God didn't. Adam did.

Rulers of Darkness

The angel told Daniel, "Your prayer got through the very first day" (Dan. 10:12). And God hears us the first day we pray, but we do have to stand sometimes before the answer comes.

It is not God who withholds answers to our prayers. He sends the answer the minute we pray. But there are forces out in the heavens endeavoring to intercept those answers.

We try to fight, wrestle, and cope with situations we see, when really there's an unseen power behind the situation. When we understand that, we'll be successful in our praying.

First John 5:19 declares, ". . . *the whole world lieth in wickedness.*" The *Amplified* translation reads, ". . . and the whole world [around us] is under the power of the evil one."

If the whole world lies in wickedness and in darkness, then the devil is ruling the whole world. The devil is ruling everybody who is unsaved. And he rules!

The devil is not ruling us, however, because the Bible says that although we are *in* the world, we are not *of* the world (John 17:16). Believers are children of light, not darkness.

The Holy Spirit is a Gentleman. He will not take any more territory than you surrender to Him. He'll not dominate you. He'll not force you.

Demons, on the other hand, use force. We read in the Bible about them driving or forcing people.

There's something here that we need to be very careful of: *Anybody who wants to drive, force, and dominate people is motivated by the spirit of the devil.* We see it in religious circles.

Colossians 1:12,13 shows that we have been delivered out of darkness.

COLOSSIANS 1:12
12 Giving thanks unto the Father, which hath made us meet [able] to be partakers of the inheritance of the saints in light.

Notice that expression "in light"!
Now notice the following verse:

COLOSSIANS 1:13
13 Who hath delivered us from the power of darkness. . . .

The Amplified Bible reads, "[The Father] has delivered and drawn us to Himself out of the control and the dominion of darkness and has transferred us into the kingdom of the Son of His love."

You see, the Father has taken us out from under the control of darkness and the rulers of darkness — the devil, demons, and evil spirits in Satan's kingdom. Ephesians 6:12 indicates the realm in which Satan's kingdom operates.

It says, ". . . *but against principalities, against powers, against the rulers of the darkness of this world, AGAINST SPIRITUAL WICKEDNESS in high places.*"

A marginal note in my *King James Version* says, "wicked spirits in the heavenlies." Three heavens are spoken of in the Bible.

Bible scholars agree that the Apostle Paul was talking about himself in Second Corinthians 12:2 when he said, *"I knew a man in Christ above fourteen years ago, (whether in the body, I cannot tell; or whether out of the body, I cannot tell: God knoweth;) such an one caught up to the third heaven."*

The first of the three heavens, right above us, is what we call the atmospheric heaven. Beyond that, out in space, are the stars — the stellar heavens. Then out beyond that is the third heaven — the Heaven of heavens — where the throne of God is.

There are wicked spirits in the atmospheric heaven above us — "in the heavenlies." We get another glimpse of this fact in the 28th chapter of Ezekiel.

The first 10 verses are a "word of the Lord," a prophetic message, given through Ezekiel to the prince of Tyrus, who was lifted up in pride. God said to him through the Prophet Ezekiel, "*. . . yet thou art a man . . .*" (Ezek. 28:2). So this prince of Tyrus was a man. Angels are not men. Evil spirits are not men.

In verses 11-19 of the same chapter, another prophetic word is given through Ezekiel, but this one is addressed to the *king* of Tyrus, a being who could not be the *prince* of Tyrus, whom God had identified earlier as a man. The king of Tyrus, therefore, must be a being, a spiritual power, a dark power, behind this kingdom.

EZEKIEL 28:11-15

11 Moreover the word of the Lord came unto me, saying,

12 Son of man, take up a lamentation upon the king of Tyrus, and say unto him, Thus saith the Lord God; Thou sealest up the sum, full of wisdom, and perfect in beauty.

13 Thou hast been in Eden the garden of God; every precious stone was thy covering, . . . the workmanship of thy tabrets and of thy pipes was prepared in thee in the day that thou wast created.

14 Thou art the anointed cherub that covereth; and I have set thee so: thou wast upon the holy mountain of

God; thou hast walked up and down in the midst of the stones of fire.
15 Thou wast perfect in thy ways from the day that thou wast created, till iniquity was found in thee.

God was talking about the devil — Lucifer — when He said, *"Thou hast been in Eden the garden of God. . . ."* The prince of Tyrus, a man, couldn't have been there. He wasn't even born. No, this "king of Tyrus" is not a man; he is a *created* being (vv. 13,15).

In these two beings — the prince of Tyrus, a man; and the king of Tyrus, Lucifer himself, a spirit being — the Bible gives the idea of a natural kingdom upon the earth dominated by a spiritual kingdom with the same name.

Everything on this earth — every human, every being — is dominated, ruled, or influenced by spirits in the unseen world. Even we as Christians are influenced and led by the Spirit of God. Romans 8:14 says, *"For as many as are led by the Spirit of God, they are the sons of God."*

If people could ever understand about this other world — this spirit world — that exists and understand that it's the world in which God lives — a world that has no beginning or end — faith would become an easy thing; a natural thing.

The reason you can count things done before they materialize is because they're already done in the spirit realm. If you'll believe they're done in this realm, they will be made manifest.

That's the reason Jesus said, *". . . What things soever ye desire, when ye pray, believe that ye receive them, and ye shall have them"* (Mark 11:24).

Now I want you to notice something that perhaps you never noticed before. Let's go back to Ephesians 6:

EPHESIANS 6:10-18
10 Finally, my brethren, be strong in the Lord, and in the power of his might.
11 Put on the whole armour of God, that ye may be able to stand against the wiles of the devil.
12 For we wrestle not against flesh and blood, but against principalities, against powers, against the rulers of the darkness of this world, against spiritual wickedness in high places.
13 Wherefore take unto you the whole armour of God, that ye may be able to withstand in the evil day, and having done all, to stand.
14 Stand therefore, having your loins girt about with truth, and having on the breastplate of righteousness;
15 And your feet shod with the preparation of the gospel of peace;
16 Above all, taking the shield of faith, wherewith ye shall be able to quench all the fiery darts of the wicked.
17 And take the helmet of salvation, and the sword of the Spirit, which is the word of God:
18 PRAYING always with all prayer and supplication in the Spirit, and watching thereunto with all perseverance and supplication for all saints.

We usually stop reading with the 17th verse. By so doing, we've taken these verses out of context. There is more truth in them than we have seen.

The object of taking on the whole armor of God is so that we can enter into the prayer life!

Putting on the armor of God and *not* entering into prayer is practically useless!

Christians entering into prayer should never forget this fact: *We have authority in the Name of Jesus against all powers of darkness!*

In the many years since I learned to really pray, I've never prayed a single prayer concerning myself or my own needs without almost instantly getting the answer.

Why? Because I know how to pray. I know what belongs to me. I know how to take authority over the devil. I know how to speak to him and tell him, "Stop your maneuvers right now!"

The Bible calls us citizens of Heaven. I know how to demand *my* rights; however, I can't always demand another person's rights for him. As an American citizen I can exercise my right to vote, but I can't exercise your right to vote. You've got to do that for yourself.

Many times people run around trying to get somebody else to pray for them. It doesn't always work. That's because they don't have the authority.

Here's where prayer comes in. We have to pray for people who don't know their rights. They may be honest, sincere, saved for years, and even filled with the Spirit, but spiritual things remain hidden to them.

When praying for others, we may have to take more time to persevere in prayer, because they may be yielding to evil spirits. Sometimes Christians yield to evil spirits and allow them to dominate them.

In praying for my own relatives, I've had to take time to persevere in prayer, standing boldly on God's Word. I've usually prayed for my relatives privately, secretly; I haven't said anything to them.

(That's our trouble: We try to deal with the individual when we ought to be dealing with the power behind the problem.)

I've simply said, "I break the power of the devil over So-and-so!"

Ephesians 6:18 speaks about making supplication "for all saints." (You see, they don't always know how to pray for themselves.)

Pleading the Case of Another

I'm convinced we have authority and power in prayer that we've never yet used. Some of us have gotten to the edge of it.

In 1947, my Sunday school superintendent, an oil field pumper, fell from on top of the pump house into the engine. The report came to me that he was dead.

When I arrived on the scene, he was lying on the ground close to the pump house. An ambulance was backed up nearby. People were all around. I knelt down beside Dr. Garrett.

He whispered to me, "I thought he was dead at first. He isn't yet, but he will die soon, and we can't move him. We'll kill him if we do."

Then the doctor said, "Reverend Hagin, take his wife aside and prepare her for this."

I took her by the arm and led her to one side — not to prepare her, however, but to pray with her.

As we moved away from the crowd, she said, "Brother Hagin, Dr. Garrett doesn't think Daddy will live, does he?"

I said, "No, he doesn't, Sister."

She said, "Isn't it wonderful that you and I have inside information?" (She meant information inside the Bible!)

I said, "Yes, thank God, we do. We'll pray and he'll live."

Well, he kept on living, wrapped in blankets, lying on the ground. Dr. Garrett remained beside him. Finally he decided to risk moving him to the hospital. I think he must have sensed we were holding him there, for he said to me, "I'm sure we'll never make it to Tyler with him alive, but we'll put him in the ambulance and try. Reverend Hagin, you get in and ride with him."

To make a long story short, he did survive the trip. Three doctors were awaiting him.

I went to the hospital and sat up with him at night. His wife stayed with him day and night.

The third night about 8 o'clock, one of the doctors said to me, "Reverend, I'll be honest with you. This is the third night and he's still in shock. We don't even know the extent of his injuries. We can't take him to the X-ray room to find out. If we move him, we'll kill him. We've done everything we know to do. He's going fast now, and there just isn't anything we can do."

Back in the room I saw that the man's wife was growing tired. (The spirit is willing, but the flesh is weak. When you grow tired physically, it's difficult for your spirit, your inward man, to continue to dominate, especially when you're looking right at the situation.) I saw her faith was waning. And I knew I had to get her out of there. I knew he would die if she stayed.

(The reason a lot of people have died is that their relatives have stayed with them! I've found out why Jesus sometimes put people out of the room when He was about to heal the sick.)

I didn't lie to her, but I didn't tell her what the doctor had told me. I said, "Now you go rest. I'll call you if there's any change here. But he'll be all right."

I had to do some spiritual wrestling that night. That is, I had to take a bold stand on the promises of God's Word. As long as I was awake and alert, my Sunday school superintendent did fine. But this was the third night I had sat up myself, and when I'd doze off in the chair, he'd begin to die.

The special duty nurse awakened me as she walked around the bed to check on him under the oxygen tent. When I first looked at him, I thought, *He's dead! I've gone to sleep and let the man die right on my hands!*

Excitedly, I asked the nurse, "Is he dead?"

"No," she said. "I thought he was. But he'll never live till I go off duty at 7 a.m." It was 2 a.m. then.

I went out into the hall, and I prayed. Very quietly, I prayed for him. I argued his case. You see, God said:

ISAIAH 43:25,26
25 I, even I, am he that blotteth out thy transgressions for mine own sake, and will not remember thy sins.
26 Put me in remembrance: let us plead together: declare thou, that thou mayest be justified.

"Put me in remembrance." God told us to remind Him of what He said. This is talking about prayer. "Declare thou." The marginal note in the *King James Version* renders this "set forth your cause." In other words, God invites us, "Plead your case."

So I simply said in a whisper at 2 a.m. out in the hospital hallway, "Lord, I'm just not going to let him die!"

And I set forth my case in front of Him.

"Number one," I said, "he's my Sunday school super-intendent. He may not be the best one in the world, but he's the best one I've ever had. He helps me. He visits the absentees. He works at it all during the week. And he helps in a number of other ways.

"Secondly, he puts 30 percent of his income into the church.

"Thirdly, he's an influence for God and for good. I've talked to businessmen downtown. They believe in him; they respect him.

"I need him. I'm the under shepherd, and You're the Great Shepherd of the Church. What I need, You need.

"Fourthly, the Bible plainly tells us death is an enemy. It's not of God. It's really of the devil. When the devil is finally eliminated, death will be eliminated from human contact. So I just rebuke death and command it to leave him. I'm not going to let him die!"

I went back into his room, sat down, and again dozed off. He started dying. I got up and went through it again, pleading his case. Actually, I went through it four times; the fourth time at 4 a.m.

At 8 o'clock, the doctor came in, pulled up the oxygen tent, and began to listen across his chest. After a little he turned to me and exclaimed, "He's come out of it! He's come out of it! You know, he might make it now! Get the stretcher! We'll take him to X-ray."

When they brought him back from X-ray, the same doctor said to me, "He's got a 50-50 chance."

I just stood there, but inside I was jumping up and down, thinking, *Fifty-fifty chance! What are you talking about, doctor? He's got a hundred percent chance to make it!* And he did make it.

Now, I never said a word to my wife or anybody else about the way I had prayed for this man. But the first time he was back in church, he testified.

First he thanked everybody for their prayers. Then he said, "Never feel sorry for anybody who dies. The last thing I remember was falling. I don't even remember hitting down in the machinery. The next conscious thing I knew was when I woke up in the hospital. And after I woke up, I never had any pain or hurt.

"But while I was unconscious, I must have died. I went up to Heaven. I heard an angelic choir. You never heard such singing in your life.

"I saw Jesus. Jesus came to me. And I was just about to fall down before Him and tell Him how much I loved Him when He said, 'You'll have to go back.'

"I said, 'I don't want to go back.'

"Jesus said, 'You'll have to go back to the earth.'

"I said, 'I don't want to go back to the earth.'

"The third time Jesus said, 'You'll have to. *Brother Hagin won't let you come.*'

"Then Jesus turned, and like you would pull a lace curtain back from a window, He pulled back a curtain and I heard Brother Hagin say, 'Lord, I'm not going to let him die.'

"Jesus said, 'See, he won't let you come.'

"The next thing I knew, I woke up in the hospital," my Sunday school superintendent concluded.

I had not told him I'd prayed that way. How did he know? The Lord let him hear me and told him that was the reason he couldn't stay in Heaven!

That got me started thinking, way back there in 1947, that we have authority to plead our case which we've never used.

I believe that at times, without realizing it, we have taken our place in our covenant in the Name of Jesus and have prayed. Without examining the Bible on the subject, we have thought, *That was a great experience the Lord helped me to have. I might not ever have another one like it.* And that kind of thinking has defeated us.

Three years later when my father-in-law lay dying in the hospital, I got to thinking about that experience with the Sunday school superintendent.

As I stood by his bedside — he was unconscious — I said, "Lord, I believe I'll just rebuke this death and command it to leave him. I believe I'll command him to live in Jesus' Name."

God said in Isaiah 43:26, "Let *us* plead *together.*" On the inside of me, the Lord plainly said to me by the Spirit, "No, don't do it. Don't you do it."

That meant I had the authority to do it!

"Leave him alone and let him die," He said. And the Lord pled his case. "First, he's 70 years old. All I've promised you is 70 or 80 years." (That is a minimum. You can go longer. If you've got more faith, claim more. But don't settle for anything less.)

"Second," He said, "he's ready to go. Spiritually, financially, he's got everything ready. He hasn't always been ready. His finances are in order; all his business is in order. He'll never have a better time to die than now. So you leave him alone and let him die."

I said, "All right, Lord, I will under one condition and one condition only. Bring him out of this death; let him revive and leave a good testimony so everybody will know where he went. Then I'll let him go."

I hadn't gotten those words out of my mouth until he opened his eyes.

"Kenneth," he said, "I'm dying."

I said, "I know it, Mr. Rooker."

He said, "Now, the sooner the better."

I said, "I know that."

He said, "You're going to get those children up here and let me see them before I go, aren't you?"

I said, "Yes, sir. I'll do it."

Our children were his only grandchildren. I phoned our pastor in Garland, Texas, and asked him to bring the children over to the hospital in Sherman. Meanwhile, I talked to the Mother Superior of this Catholic hospital and asked about bringing small children in.

She said, "Don't pay attention to any rules. That man should have been dead two days ago. We can't understand how he's lived. Bring in anybody you want to — it's just a miracle that he's revived."

So his family, including the little grandchildren, gathered around his bed. And you'd have thought he was going on a vacation the next day. He never shed a tear. The nurses rolled up the head of his bed, and he sat there laughing and talking.

The next day he lapsed into unconsciousness and started dying. I stood at the foot of the bed just as death fastened its final throes upon him.

Suddenly his eyes popped open. He saw me and said, "My God, Kenneth, I'm dying."

I said, "I know, Mr. Rooker, but you're not afraid to go."

"No," he said. "I'm not afraid."

I said, "Lie back on the pillow and let 'er go."

He lay back, smiled, relaxed, and a light flashed across his face as he took off. Praise God! (You've got to have faith to live — but you've got to have faith to die, too.)

It is possible to pray and get answers sometimes which are not always the wisest and the best.

We need to use wisdom — because we do have authority. I've learned that from experience. I know it from the Word.

According to the Word, many times what we say, He will do — because we've got the authority down here.

I am satisfied that if we will just walk in the light of God's Word and pray, we can change the lives of our loved ones and the situations around us.

We've seen from the life of Daniel, who prevailed in prayer standing on God's Word, that the course of a nation can be changed through prayer. We've also seen examples of how we can prevail in prayer using God's Word to plead the case of another.

Not every need can be met through offering a short, one-time prayer. Sometimes it is necessary to persevere in prayer by taking a bold stand on God's Word, refusing to back down until the answer comes.

Chapter 24
Praying for Your Nation

I exhort therefore, that, first of all, supplications, prayers, intercessions, and giving of thanks, be made for all men; For kings, and for all that are in authority; that we may lead a quiet and peaceable life in all godliness and honesty. For this is good and acceptable in the sight of God our Saviour; Who will have all men to be saved, and to come unto the knowledge of the truth.

— 1 Timothy 2:1-4

After the final service of our Campmeeting '79, some of the speakers and others went up to Kenneth Hagin Jr.'s hotel suite for sandwiches.

As we were talking about the things of God, the Spirit of God kept moving on me. (Actually, only three times in my life has the Spirit moved on me in such a measure.)

I said to the others, "Let's pray. The Spirit of God keeps moving on me."

We prayed. By the Spirit, I ministered to each one present. Then I was caught up in the spirit of prayer. For lack of a better term, I was "lost in the spirit." I was not unconscious — but I was more conscious of spiritual things. Spiritual things were more real than the natural.

I sat with my eyes shut, praying in tongues, for what proved to be several hours. (It was just after midnight when we started praying. When it was all over, and I opened my eyes, it was after 4 a.m. Yet it seemed as if it had been only 10 or 15 minutes.)

The Lord spoke to me. Among other things, He gave me instructions concerning the Prayer and Healing School we are now holding every weekday on the RHEMA Bible Training Center campus.

And I saw something. I saw three things coming up out of the Atlantic Ocean. They looked like three giant black frogs as large as whales. One was in midair. The other two had just stuck their heads up out of the water from the east.

I had seen something similar nine years before.

Jesus said to me, "You saw the same thing in 1970. I told you then exactly what they were, but you didn't do what you should have done about it. I told you back in 1970 to pray for the leaders of the nation. What happened [Watergate and so forth] isn't all the fault of the man who was then President. I am going to hold the Christians of this nation responsible. You are the ones who allowed what happened to your nation. If you had prayed, it never would have happened. I showed you what was about to happen. Go back and check. . . ."

(Later, I went back and checked what the Lord had said to me in 1970 from tapes and manuscripts of a special meeting we held in October 1970.)

Jesus said to me, "Back in 1970, you saw three similar dark objects come up out of the Atlantic and leapfrog all the way across the land. If you and the Christians had done what you should have done, none of those things would have happened to your nation. You would not have had the riots. You would not have had the political disturbances. Your President would not have made the mistakes he made. In fact, I am holding the Church responsible for his mistakes."

I began to weep and cry, "Oh, God!"

"Yes," He said, "I am holding you and the Church responsible."

Then He said, "When you tell that to some of the Christians, they will laugh. But when they stand before my judgment seat and they receive the condemnation rather than the man who was then President, they won't laugh.

"If Christians had done what I told them to do in the Bible — if they had prayed for the leaders of their nation — they would have kept the evil spirits from operating."

Then He continued, "Similar things — not the same things — but similar things are about to happen again. If you do not pray, they will happen. I am not going to hold the President responsible for the nation; I am going to hold the Christians of the nation responsible."

Now, let me explain something — you have to know how to interpret these things. I saw those three creatures come up out of the Atlantic Ocean. But that doesn't mean they rise out of the ocean. From Genesis to Revelation "seas" and "waters" refer to a multitude of people. Out of the multitude of people, these things will rise up. Sinners are dominated by the devil; they're in his kingdom.

Jesus said, "There will arise, unless the Christians pray, not for the same purpose that the other riots came — but there will be riots, tumults, and disturbances all across the nation.

"Second, something is about to happen to the Presi-

Jude 13 false teachers
No where in the index do I see "waters" referring to people

dent that should not happen — and will not happen if you will pray.

"Third, something is about to happen again that will bring further trouble in the economic scene, the financial structure.

"But you can stop all three. You can stop the upheaval in the social structure. You can stop the upheaval and the activity of the devil in the political scene. You can stop the devil from disrupting the financial scene of your nation.

"You can change all three through intercessory prayer. That's one of the main purposes for the classes you are going to start in the fall."

First Things First

God gave us specific instructions to put first things first.

"Yes, but," people have said to me, "I'll tell you, as long as the Democrats are in, it's not going to go." Others have said, "As long as the Republicans are in. . . ."

If you are party minded first, you will never amount to much of a Christian. Christians are to put first things first.

The Word says, *"I exhort therefore, that, first of all . . ."* (1 Tim. 2:1).

First! Before you pray for your children, before you pray for me, before I pray for you, *". . . first of all, supplications, prayers, intercessions, and giving of thanks, be made for all men; For kings, and for all that are in authority . . ."* (1 Tim. 2:1-2).

So we would know who the "all men" are, it says, *"For*

kings, and for all that are in authority . . ." (v. 2).

First of all, we are to pray for our leaders — for all those who are in authority in national government, state or provincial government, and on down to city government.

Why? Go on reading. . . .

". . . that we may lead a quiet and peaceable life in all godliness and honesty" (v. 2). That "we" as Christians may lead a quiet and peaceable life. God is interested in us.

All the kings Paul was instructing them to pray for were not born again.

Will God bless leaders even though they are not saved?

Certainly. The Spirit of God would not tell us to pray for something we could not have. That would be stupid.

Why will He bless them? For one thing, He is interested in us.

"For this is good and acceptable in the sight of God our Saviour" (1 Tim. 2:3). It is good and acceptable in the sight of God our Savior that we pray first of all for all who are in authority. It is good and acceptable in the sight of God our Savior that we lead a quiet and peaceable life.

"Who will have all men to be saved, and to come unto the knowledge of the truth" (v. 4). When there is war — when there is upheaval — when there is turmoil — it is difficult to spread the Gospel. But when there is peace — when there is tranquility — then we are free to go and spread the Gospel.

No wonder the devil wants to attack the United

States, for instance. You can go around the world and you will find that 90 percent of all missionary work is done from America. If the devil could stop us, he could stop the flow of God's blessings.

But, blessed be God, he cannot do it!

How are we told to pray for those in authority?

" . . . *supplications, prayers, intercessions, and giving of thanks* . . ." (1 Tim. 2:1).

We have examples in Scripture of those who successfully prayed for cities and nations.

One such Bible example is Abraham who prayed for two cities — Sodom and Gomorrah. Read that account in Genesis chapter 18.

The Lord said, ". . . *Shall I hide from Abraham that thing which I do*" (v. 17).

He would not destroy those wicked cities without informing His blood-covenant friend.

Abraham was standing on his blood-covenant rights when he said to the Lord, ". . . *Wilt thou also destroy the righteous with the wicked? Peradventure there be fifty righteous within the city: wilt thou also destroy and not spare the place for the fifty righteous that are therein? That be far from thee to do after this manner, to slay the righteous with the wicked: and that the righteous should be as the wicked, that be far from thee: Shall not the Judge of all the earth do right?*" (vv. 23-25).

The Lord said, ". . . *If I find in Sodom fifty righteous within the city, then I will spare all the place for THEIR sakes*" (v. 26).

Remember what First Timothy 2:2 said, ". . . *that WE may lead a quiet and peaceable life*. . . ."

God said He would spare the whole city for the sake of 50 righteous.

Abraham kept going down in number until he said to the Lord, ". . . *Peradventure ten shall be found there* . . ." (Gen. 18:32)

And the Lord said, ". . . *I will not destroy it for ten's sake*" (v. 32).

Consider the terrible sins that existed in Sodom — yet God said He would spare the whole place for ten's sake.

You know, this old world would already have been destroyed if it were not for us Christians. Jesus said, "*Ye are the salt of the earth* . . ." (Matt. 5:13).

I am old enough to remember before we had electric refrigerators. My grandfather killed hogs. He'd put salt on the meat to preserve it.

This world is bad enough — but if it were not for us Christians, it would certainly be rotten.

God told Abraham He would spare the cities for the sake of ten righteous. There are more than ten righteous persons in America today.

Some say, "We're going to pot."

No, we're not!

Don't listen to such talk as that.

I believe there are people in America today who will take their place in prayer just as Abraham did.

Abraham didn't sit around and talk about how wicked they were and how they were all going to hell. *He interceded on their behalf!*

If we will take our place, we can change things.

We have a better covenant based on better promises!

I was in the home of a minister of the Gospel whose 4-year-old son misbehaved so much that he embarrassed me, and even embarrassed my son, who was also 4. Ken said to me the minute we got into the car, "That boy is awful, isn't he?"

He talked terribly to his father. When his father picked him up in his arms, petting him a little to quieten him down, the boy slapped his cheeks and said, "You old liar. What you're telling is not so. You're a liar."

This pastor — Full Gospel, Spirit-filled — said to me, "Well, you know, the Bible says that in the last days, children will be disobedient to parents."

"Yes," I said, "the Bible also says that the love of many shall wax cold, but that doesn't mean my love has to wax cold. And that doesn't mean my children are going to be disobedient to their parents."

You can sit around and say, "Well, the Bible says that evil men and seducers will wax worse and worse, deceived and being deceived. This whole thing is going down. The love of many shall wax cold," and if you just dwell on that side, you will grow cold. The devil will take you over and all your children.

But, you don't have to think along that line.

Wake up and realize who you are in Christ. The gates of hell shall not prevail against the Church! Jesus is the Head of the Church — not Satan. Jesus is bigger than the devil. In fact, He already has defeated him. He arose victorious over him — and His victory is my victory.

Think in line with God's Word and realize that no matter what the situation, we can do something about it.

EZEKIEL 22:30,31
30 And I sought for a man among them, that should make up the hedge, and stand in the gap before me for the land, that I should not destroy it: but I found none.
31 Therefore have I poured out mine indignation upon them; I have consumed them with the fire of my wrath: their own way have I recompensed upon their heads. . . .

This is God talking. Abraham interceded for two cities. Here God is talking about an entire nation. If He could have found ONE man who would have stood in the gap, who would have interceded on behalf of the nation, judgment would not have come.

"Well," someone might ask, "if God really wanted to spare the land, why didn't He just go ahead and do it anyhow? Isn't He God? If that's His will, why doesn't He go ahead and do it?"

Go back to First Timothy 2:4. There it says that God wills that all men come unto the knowledge of the truth. Why doesn't He just go ahead and make them all be born again? If He can do anything He wants to do, why doesn't He do it? Why does He wait for somebody to intercede?

We discussed this in detail in Chapter One, "Why Pray?"

Satan became the god of this world until Adam's lease runs out. He is not my god — I am not of this world. But he is responsible for the wars between nations, the murders, the violence that is done in the world.

God will not transgress His own Word. He gave the lease to Adam. Adam gave it to the devil. It is running out. But until that time, God can only intervene as

Christians seek His face and ask Him to move.

Satan's authority over matters on the earth can only be overcome as Christians pray in behalf of their country. God is longing today for someone who will make up the hedge and stand in the gap before Him for the land.

Prayer can be offered in your known tongue. It can also be offered in other tongues as the Holy Spirit helps you. Ask the Holy Spirit to help you, and *continue* to pray.

Here is where some people miss it. They don't hear everything you teach, and they grab some little something and run off with it. There are some things you can pray the prayer of faith on — and you pray one prayer and that's the end of it. You don't have to pray anymore; you just thank God for the answer. You can do that for salvation, for the baptism in the Holy Spirit, for healing — for anything God promised right now. But there are other things you cannot pray the prayer of faith on. One of them is this matter of praying for our nation. You must *continue* in prayer for the leaders of your nation.

Chapter 25
Excesses

In the Bible, particularly in Old Testament times, people were set apart or consecrated to a sacred office by the anointing of oil. Oil was a type of the Holy Spirit. The Holy Spirit would come upon men and women to anoint them to stand in a particular office. In the New Testament, God is still anointing His people. Not everyone in the Body of Christ is called and anointed of God to one of the fivefold ministry gifts. But every Christian is called and anointed of God to reign and rule as a king and priest in this life.

REVELATION 1:6
6 And [God] hath made us kings and priests unto God and his Father; to him be glory and dominion for ever and ever. Amen.

REVELATION 5:10
10 And [God] hast made us unto our God kings and priests: and we shall reign on the earth.

When you think about priests, you immediately think about a go-between. The priest is a "go-between"; one who prays to God on behalf of people, and that's where we come in today. We are to go into the Presence of God for those who are hindered in going to God, or for those who don't know they can go to God themselves.

We must remember that the devil thrives on ignorance. Ignorant of God's Word, some Christians fall into the error of spiritual pride, thinking: *We're a special*

*class of people. We have a special ministry, and a special
calling; no one else is like us.* That's exactly what the
devil wants. That's the same way he sinned. Lucifer was
lifted up in pride. Instead of getting elevated about it, we
need to take the attitude: Thank God, we are all
anointed to be priests; let's get after it!

> **1 PETER 2:5,9**
> **5   Ye also, as lively stones, are built up a spiritual
> house, an holy priesthood** [that's all of us; the whole Body
> of Christ!], **to offer up spiritual sacrifices, acceptable to
> God by Jesus Christ. . . .**
> **9   But ye are a chosen generation, a royal priesthood,
> an holy nation, a peculiar people; that ye should shew
> forth the praises of him who hath called you out of
> darkness into his marvellous light.**

You see how far people can get off on some of these
issues. Actually, prayer is not a *special* calling — everyone in the Body of Christ is to pray because God has
anointed every one of us to be priests unto our God. The
whole Body of Christ has been called out of darkness
into light and is a part of this royal priesthood, not just a
chosen few. Some have responded more readily to the
Holy Spirit and entered into it more than others, but
prayer belongs to every born-again Christian.

Because people think they have some *special calling,*
they think they have to *perform.* So they try to do something in the flesh instead of waiting on the anointing.
People get off into error when they take spiritual things
out of context. Some are even going around saying they
stand in the "office of the intercessor." They say this
"office" puts them on the same level as the minister or

pastor, so that gives them the right to tell the pastor what to do! In the first place, there is no such thing as the "office" of intercessor. We find the fivefold offices or ministry gifts which *God set in the Church,* listed in Ephesians 4:11,12:

EPHESIANS 4:11,12
11 And he gave some, apostles; and some, prophets; and some, evangelists; and some, pastors and teachers;
12 For the perfecting of the saints, for the work of the ministry, for the edifying of the body of Christ.

We can readily see that prayer is not mentioned here in Ephesians. That's because praying is not a ministry gift. We need to keep spiritual matters in their rightful place, and not get them out of place. Also, we need to clarify what we mean when we say that prayer is a *ministry.* If we are using the word "ministry" in a general sense, that's one thing. Generally speaking, anything you do for God is a ministry. In that case, prayer could be considered as a *ministry,* just as anything we do for God is a ministry — a service — unto God. But if we are speaking specifically, using the word "ministry" as one of the fivefold ministry gifts given to the Church, then, no, prayer is not a *ministry.* Praying is not a ministry gift.

1 CORINTHIANS 12:28
28 And God hath set some in the church, first apostles, secondarily prophets, thirdly teachers, after that miracles, then gifts of healings, HELPS, governments, diversities of tongues.

If we are using "ministry" in a general sense, then prayer would have to come under the ministry of helps.

The saints are not perfected through prayer. Yes, we can pray for people, help and bless them, but that doesn't *perfect* them. Ephesians 4:11,12 says that the offices of the apostle, prophet, evangelist, pastor, and teacher are for the *perfecting* of the saints. If it took prayer to perfect the saints, the Bible would have mentioned prayer or praying as a ministry gift. No, prayer *helps* people.

Secondly, the ministry of helps is not on the same level as the fivefold ministry gifts. The ministry of helps includes anything that helps or assists those in the fivefold ministry function as they should.

Intercession With Groanings

ROMANS 8:26
26 Likewise the Spirit also helpeth our infirmities: for we know not what we should pray for as we ought: but the Spirit itself [Himself] maketh intercession for us with groanings which cannot be uttered.

Another excess that has arisen in prayer, is this issue of *groanings*. Many times people try to carry out spiritual things in the natural and in the flesh. God *anoints* His people to carry out His will and purposes, but when people get over into the flesh, they get into trouble. It's one thing to groan under the anointing of the Holy Spirit. But on the other hand, you can do all the groaning in the flesh you want to, but without the anointing you are not going to produce anything. When the Holy Spirit moves on you to pray "with groanings which cannot be uttered," there will be results! The problem is people are trying to mimic and imitate the Holy Spirit and they get off into error.

Questions and Answers

Some have asked, "Is it possible to groan in the Spirit as an act of the will?" There's no Scripture for groaning as an act of the will. The Bible says, ". . . *the Spirit itself* [Himself] *maketh intercession for us with groanings . . .*" (Rom. 8:26). Sometimes people just naturally groan because they are burdened, and it's not the Holy Spirit at all. But it's another thing when the Spirit takes hold. I've found that praising and worshipping God many times leads into this realm where the Spirit of God begins to take hold together with your spirit in groanings. But you can't just do it yourself — that's the point I'm trying to get over to you.

People ask, "Can a person travail as an act of the will?" Paul said in Galatians 4:19: *"My little children, of whom I travail in birth again until Christ be formed in you."* Paul uses the same term as a woman in travail to birth a child. Can a woman travail as an act of her will? No! If there's no child to bring forth, she could try to travail but nothing would come of it. The Spirit of God brings us into travail because He knows there's something there to give birth to. For example, some people are saved because they hear the Word of God and believe it. But there are others who will never be saved unless someone travails for them. We don't know who they are; only the Spirit of God knows.

Can you travail to birth something anytime you want? Well, could a woman give birth to a baby anytime she wants? No, she has to be pregnant first. Can travail be loosed upon people by the laying on of hands? No, that's laying empty hands on empty heads. Is groaning more effective than praying in tongues? Certainly not. So much of what we do, if we're not careful, is in the flesh! And sometimes it is a mixture of the flesh and the Spirit.

Of course you can stir yourself up in prayer at any time. And there are times when prayer takes strenuous effort. I've stirred myself up to seek God, and then the Holy Spirit took hold with me. And we do have a scriptural basis for this because the Word of God says, *". . . stir up the gift of God, which is in thee . . . "* (2 Tim. 1:6).

We need to remember that we need all kinds of praying, not just one kind. Don't misunderstand me; thank God for intercession. But the Bible says, *"Praying always with all prayer . . ."* (Eph. 6:18), or as one translation says, "Praying with all kinds of prayer." So we need all kinds of prayer. Let's learn to be sensitive to the Holy Spirit, and see which way He is moving at the moment and what direction He wants to take. Then let's just follow Him!

Chapter 26
Reviving the Art

The art of prayer, which includes intercession and supplication, has been virtually lost in the Church. Early-day Pentecostals knew something about it. Second-generation Pentecostals knew a little about it. Third-generation Pentecostals know almost nothing about it. Charismatics know almost nothing about it.

But for God to accomplish what He desires to accomplish in the '90s, the art of prayer will have to be resurrected.

When I first received the baptism in the Holy Spirit and came over among Pentecostal people, I accepted the pastorate of a small Full Gospel church in the black land of North Central Texas. Most of the congregation were farmers.

In the fall of the year when they harvested cotton, we dismissed all services except for Saturday night, Sunday morning, and Sunday night. On Sunday afternoons, we'd bring something to eat and gather at someone's house to eat together.

This particular Sunday we met at my future wife's house. A dear little lady was there. I had heard of her, but had never met her. Everyone called her Mother Howard. They referred to her as "a mother in Israel."

She ate. But as soon as we finished eating, and were visiting, she asked for a room where she could get off by herself. She knelt on the bare floor. (I learned that sometimes she would put a newspaper on the floor and lay her forehead on it as she prayed all Sunday afternoon without moving.)

She was a widow. She owned her own home in a neighboring community. A pastor I knew lived in one side of her home with his wife and child.

He said to me, "She makes a business of prayer. She arises at 4 in the morning. She prays from 4 to 8 every morning. Then she cooks her a little bite to eat. After that she puts in another two hours praying. She eats a light lunch, then she usually comes over to our side of the house and visits with us a while. By 2 or 3 in the afternoon she goes back to prayer. Sometimes she prays until midnight. If the burden is there, she prays all night."

She was born again many years ago in Dallas. Then they had moved to a town where there was no Full Gospel church. In fact, there was no Full Gospel church in any city or town around about.

One by one, town by town, city by city, she took them, and prayed until a church was built there. Then she took the next town, and prayed until a church was built there.

Mother Howard, that little old woman, that beautiful saint of God, prayed a church into every town, every village, and every nook of North Texas.

I've thought about how it might be when we all get to Heaven and the rewards are passed out. The pastors who built the churches will be ready to step up and get their reward, but Jesus is going to call Mother Howard up there!

Hers was the work that got the job done! No one saw her. They hardly knew she existed. But she didn't wile her time away visiting and talking on Sunday afternoons. She was on the job. She literally gave her life for others.

That's what Jesus did. And He is calling for those who will give themselves to prayer today.